Dales

' ... when I try to imagine a faultless love
   Or the life to come, what I hear is the murmur
Of underground streams, what I see is a limestone landscape.'

In Praise of Limestone, W H Auden

For Louise

published by
pocket mountains ltd
Holm Street, Moffat DG10 9EB
pocketmountains.com

ISBN 13: 9-780955-4548-1-3

Printed in Poland

Introduction

Windswept felltops, ancient ruins, tranquil riverside meadows and the singular beauty of sculptured limestone – the Yorkshire Dales is an iconic English landscape, and one of the country's best places to explore on foot. From the grandeur of the Three Peaks and spectacular Malham to the lonely heights above Wensleydale and the sleepy dales of the north and west, this guide blends an eye for the overlooked and unfrequented with a fresh perspective on the more familiar corners of the National Park.

There are forty circular routes here, gathered for varying reasons: some are dramatic and some are soothing, some are variations on the established classics and some are constructed with solitude in mind, some meander through valleys and some traverse the highest hills, some are charmed by natural beauty and some challenged by history's gritty legacy; all, though, open a window on to a better understanding of the Dales, its landscape, its past and its people.

About this guide
This guide splits the Dales into five areas: Nidderdale and Wharfedale; Malham, Littondale and Upper Wharfedale; The Three Peaks and Ribblesdale; From the Howgills to Hawes; Lower Wensleydale and Swaledale. These are based on the obvious geographical cues, but also on settlements and access. Each area has its own personality within the Dales family, though transitions and the natural variations within

the personalities themselves make the drawing of lines a slightly arbitrary exercise. Suffice to say, all have elements as worthwhile as anything in the Dales and all demand your attention.

Most of these routes are intended as a comfortable day or vigorous half-day and involve a reasonable amount of ascent and descent. Some lengthy ones will occupy fully the light of a winter day, while a few are more compressed and hint at summer evenings or Sunday afternoons. Each route sets out at its beginning the distance and height gained, the relevant Ordnance Survey (OS) 1:25000 map (which should always be carried) and an indication of the walking time it will take. Duration will always be a moot point with plenty of variables in play: fit, experienced walkers in spring sunshine will cover the same ground quicker than the infirm in a downpour. So, take it as a rough guide intended to assist with planning your day, and bear in mind it does not allow for any of the stops that you may have in mind. The route map is also a general guide and is emphatically not intended for navigation.

Getting around
As a lightly-populated, rural upland area, the Dales is a challenge for the public transport providers, with the best walking sometimes isolated from the main arteries. I would always encourage the reader to use public transport where feasible (yorkshiretravel.net for more information), and there are some

good local bus services – and in the west the Settle-Carlisle Railway – but I have not slavishly allowed these to dictate the start/finish points of the routes chosen. The best of the Dales sometimes eludes the bus driver's steady hand and sure foot! When shackled to the car ideally use one of the main car parks – often the start point will anyway steer you in that direction. Again, that is not always an option, but a recognised parking area should be. In the rare cases where I suggest on-street parking, please do so considerately – be wary of congesting narrow village streets and of blocking gateways, lanes and passing places: if in doubt, don't.

Environment

This is a sensitive environment and in the words of John Muir, 'take only photographs, leave only footprints'. Multiplied by millions those footprints bring their own problems, of course, and there is plenty of evidence of erosion control on paths throughout the National Park, especially around the Three Peaks. Much of this is effective, sensitive and practical – every time alien stone or duck boarding makes your heart sink, there will be another time when you are glad for the measures – so please play your part, too: where a footpath exists stick to it, rather than its fringe, walking single file if necessary. Use stiles and gates where they exist and avoid leaving litter at all costs ('pack it in, pack it out', as the Americans say). Get to grips with the Countryside and

Moorland Visitor's Codes. Keep dogs under control, ideally on a lead, especially when close to livestock and farms or on the moors during the breeding season for ground-nesting birds (1 March – 31 July). Never come between a cow and her calf (with or without dog). During lambing time, farmers are particularly and understandably sensitive – remember this is a working landscape; a little respect goes a long way. All this (common sense, really) helps to sustain a harmonious relationship between visitors and locals.

Safety

This guide assumes a degree of familiarity with the particular magic of remote fells in inclement weather. The hills of the Yorkshire Dales are hardly menacing but sudden weather changes, mist, cold and rain are as dangerous here as in any upland area. Never underestimate how much more hostile the tops can be than the valleys, even in summer. You need to have the wherewithal to use a map and compass and to be otherwise properly equipped with waterproofs, warm clothing, food and water. Decent hillwalking boots are essential, as are knowing your own limitations and carrying the right OS map – in the end, most Mountain Rescue calls come down to slips, exhaustion or simply getting lost. A mobile phone is a good idea, but not a panacea in the ills of an emergency – you might not get reception. Always have on you a torch, first-aid kit, whistle and watch. Check the weather forecast before you leave and ensure someone knows where you are going and when you are due to return. Finally, if you stray remember that disused mine-shafts, sink holes, pots and peat bogs dot the moors of the Dales – watch where you place your feet!

If all this implies that walking in the area is an ordeal to be endured, be assured it is not. If you have the confidence of sound preparation, knowledge and equipment, you can ensure that your happy expedition will remain just that, even when the weather turns, as at some point it inevitably will.

Access

The legal 'right to roam' applied locally in May 2005 under the Countryside and Rights of Way Act (2000) opens up new routes to walkers that may have previously been closed off, adding to existing rights of access in the Yorkshire Dales. Indeed, that right is exercised to a lesser or greater extent in a

significant number of these walks.

Under the Act, the public has new rights of access on foot to areas classified as open country (mountain, moor, heath and down) and registered common land for recreational use. The right does not extend to activities such as cycling, canoeing, horse-riding or camping, though existing rights may already be in place for these activities on some land.

There are other restrictions in the Act: for instance, walkers must not damage any wall, fence, hedge, stile or gate in exercising their right of access, certain types of land are exempt and landowners have the right to limit access temporarily (check at one of the National Park Centres in Grassington, Malham, Hawes, Aysgarth or Reeth).

It is worth familiarising yourself with the legislation and what it means for walking in the area. The Ramblers' Association can provide more details through their website (ramblers.org.uk/freedom).

Nidderdale and Wharfedale

Wharfedale both benefits and suffers from its proximity to Harrogate, Ilkley and the conurbations of West Yorkshire. This is affluent, gastro-pub country with a sheen of quiet gentility, popular with second homers, commuters and daytrippers, and in danger, perhaps, of losing touch with its robust agricultural heritage. That accessibility means there is no shortage of visitors, and Grassington in particular moves to a touristy beat, but it is not hard to find peace away from the villages. The appeal of the landscape is easy to see: from moor to wood, lane and river there is a friendly, rolling beauty, with just a hint of the wild in the air. Bookended by Bolton Abbey and Kilnsey Crag there is also a notable, compressed variety – it is quite easy to incorporate limestone and gritstone, felltop and valley meadow in an afternoon. The routes here reflect those easy transitions.

Why Nidderdale is not included within the National Park is anybody's guess, though the residents no doubt do not complain when visitors shoot by on their way to better-known Wharfedale. Now designated an Area of Outstanding Natural Beauty, it is the reservoirs that dominate, especially the remarkable Scar House and Angram dams at the head of the valley, which are as worthy of a visit as anything in the Dales. In the meantime, though, let us keep it our secret.

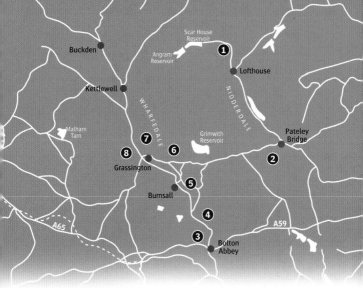

1 **The waters of Nidderdale** 8
Marvel at the soaring dams, tranquil riverside meadows and wild moors of Upper Nidderdale

2 **A Pateley Bridge folly** 10
An unusual journey up and down the undulating – and overlooked – woods and lanes above Pateley Bridge

3 **The heights above Bolton Abbey** 12
Experience two sides of the Dales, from the throng at Bolton Abbey to the solitude of Middle Hare Head

4 **On Simon's Seat** 14
This famed beacon and the infamous Strid make for a classic Wharfedale round, both high and low

5 **Into Barguest's lair** 16
If you dare, search for the mysterious and shadowy Troller's Gill. But first, a glorious riverside stroll

6 **Ghosts on the moor** 18
Just like the workers once did, approach Grassington's long-deceased lead mining industry by Hebden Gill

7 **Finding Mossdale Scar** 20
Set out on a moorland expedition from Grassington, returning by the airy terrace above Conistone to Lea Green

8 **Ancient lanes above Wharfedale** 22
Superb, ever-changing views open along an exploration of the byways above this most celebrated dale

◀ Kilnsey Crag looms

The waters of Nidderdale

Walk time 7h **Height gain** 390m
Distance 23km **OS Map** Explorer OL30
(or Explorer 298)

**Enjoy a splendid day following the
River Nidd to the dark, brooding dams
of Scar House and Angram. A round of
Scar House Reservoir is then capped
with a stride along a high-level return.**

Start at the small public car park in the
centre of Lofthouse (GR101734). Walk
north out of the village along the road for
200m to a walled lane on the left (SP Scar
House Reservoir). This (very pretty) lane
leads past lush pastures and shady copses
for 1.4km to Thrope Farm, then for a further
250m. Drop down to the side of the river

(which is often dried up), crossing 250m on.
Follow the path around to Limley Farm:
enter the yard of the left-hand farmhouse
and go through the metal gate in the far
corner. Pick up a path that sticks close to
the river, before cutting across two wide
pastures. Approaching the far wall in the
second (with a barn beyond), cross a
footbridge back to the opposite bank. Press
on upstream for 1.75km to the far side of
the farm buildings at Low Woodale. Turn
left, cross the bridge and ascend the track
to the reservoir road. Head uphill by road
for 200m, then turn on to a hard, level
track peeling right. After 600m go through
a gate to the right on to a track into a
conifer plantation. The dam now soars

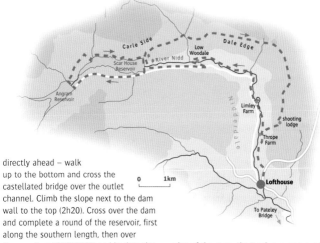

directly ahead – walk up to the bottom and cross the castellated bridge over the outlet channel. Climb the slope next to the dam wall to the top (2h20). Cross over the dam and complete a round of the reservoir, first along the southern length, then over Angram Dam (GR044762) and back to the north. (On the return the path initially heads northeast for 1km, before descending to just above the waterline.) Back at its northern tip (4h), climb away from Scar House Dam on a track, switching back to the right (ENE) after 100m (SP Lofthouse). The way ascends gradually, then drops to round a gully, before rising again to a shooting lodge (4h50). Walk north for 100m to join stony Dale Edge track, proceeding at first east. As it follows the

edge of the moor the track curves around to the south, giving splendid views over the valley and reservoirs. Eventually, 4.5km after the previous shooting lodge, another is reached, with a distinctive tower bearing the letter 'R' (GR107753) (6h20). Descend sharply by it, west to a gate in the lower wall. Beyond, traverse the steep slope southwest and descend through the fields below to Thrope Farm. Rejoining the lane from Lofthouse, head south back into the village (7h).

A tale of two reservoirs

The twinkling waters of Angram and Scar House Reservoirs supply the Bradford metropolitan area. Angram, tucked beneath Great and Little Whernside, was completed in 1919, with construction of its much larger sibling beginning two years later. Scar House Dam proved to be a major undertaking – at the time it was the largest masonry dam in Europe (over one million tons of stone were used). The workforce was housed in a temporary village beneath the dam that included a hospital, school and cinema. All were demolished when the project was finally completed in 1936.

◄ Scar House Dam

A Pateley Bridge folly

Walk time 3h20 Height gain 370m
Distance 11km OS Map Explorer 298

**A gentle exploration of the rolling
moors, woods and lanes above
Pateley Bridge, taking in the notable
Yorke's Folly.**

Start at the car park by the Nidderdale
showground, Pateley Bridge (GR157654).
Walk south from the town, turning up the
first road on the left (opposite the Royal
Oak pub). At the fringe of Bewerley, make
the sharp turn right onto a minor road. After
150m, cross the stile to the footpath on the
left (SP Toft Gate); crest tiny Sugar Hill and
drop down to the woods. Follow the path
beside the beck to the languid fishpond,
then fork right (south) to a single-track road.

Turn right, descending to the foot of the rise
(just past a bridge). Go through the gate
into the woods, cross the beck and keep
with the path as it ascends broadly
southeast to the far edge of the trees.
At the junction with the Nidderdale Way,
cut back to the right on a broad path to the
top of the wood (passing to the left of a
subterranean construction) and on to
another road. Cross over to the wide path
leading quickly to Yorke's Folly (GR157635)
(1h). Return to the road, cross back over and
trace a route west over the moor to a
ravine. A sharp descent along a narrow but
distinct path leads to a footbridge. Climb
back through the bracken on the far slope
to meet a ladder stile over the wall to the
right. Cross back into Skrikes Wood, picking

◀ Pastoral charm above Bewerley

up a faint path north. In descent, shadow the wall to the left to reach a gate, further up the single-track road left earlier. Now work up the steady gradient of the road for 800m to just before the crest. Turn down the driveway for Gillbeck House to the right (by the Wildlife Trust sign), following it to the right of the buildings. Keep to the path indicated between fences. Beyond the gate drop down to the right, aiming for the gate to the northwest; now continue in the same direction across three further fields to the B6265 (2h10). Cross to the stile opposite, picking up a wall to the right providing an

infallible guide northwest to Ivin Waite. Join a track running into a walled lane down to a junction with a private road. Turn right and follow this lovely, gently rising and falling lane, which serves only a handful of scattered properties. After 1.6km the lane dives into woods and passes the rambling Eagle Hall. Continue down to the B6265 and over to the lane opposite. Soon enough pass the stile crossed at the beginning of the walk; it is now a case of simply retracing steps back to the (comparative) bustle of Pateley (3h20).

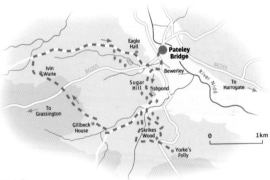

For a loaf and a shilling

Yorke's Folly was the result of an early 19th-century 'workfare' scheme. Conceived by John Yorke to keep his labourers at Bewerley Hall busy and employed during a lean time (for which they each received a loaf and a shilling per day), the folly served no purpose other than to exude a vaguely gothic, monastic air – which it does well. There were originally three columns – one collapsed in storms in 1893, after which the local name changed from 'Three Stoops' to 'Two Stoops'.

The heights above Bolton Abbey

Middle Hare Head (302m) Walk time 3h
Height gain 225m Distance 11km
OS Map Explorer OL2

The ruins and riverside at Bolton Abbey must be on just about every 'to do' list for the Dales – this one is no different. But first, experience the unfrequented, windswept heights to the west.

Start at Bolton Abbey car park (GR070539). Cross the B6160 and walk through the archway in the abbey perimeter wall by the tearoom. Drop down to the River Wharfe and turn south, following the riverside to Bolton Bridge. Back on tarmac, turn right and go along the road around the Devonshire Arms Hotel. Cross back over the B6160 and walk down the old road heading away from the hotel (which soon narrows). After 500m, cross over a stile just beyond a wall on the right and walk up the slope to three trees on the horizon. Keep in the same direction to Hesketh Farm, skirting to the right of the buildings. Now, turning left, follow the unclassified road for 2km into Halton East (1h15). Just past the village institute turn right on to Moor Lane, continuing up the track as the road ends.

It is an easy, steady climb. At the head of the lane turn right along a stone path that leads quickly to the Embsay-Barden road. Superb views now extend over Lower Barden Reservoir and northeast to Simon's Seat. Cross the cattle grid and go through the gate to the right (SP Bolton Abbey). Head east along the top of the ridge over Middle Hare Head (GR049553) (1h45), before descending close to the left of a wall over Little Hare Head. Beyond the next gate descend southeast to the edge of woods, then zigzag down the path between the trees. Emerging, take the left-hand gate of the two at the end of the first field. Pass to the left of some ponds and descend towards the now visible castellations of

Bolton Hall. At the road, turn left, and keep to the (very) narrow pavement for 100m to the northern entrance of the priory. Explore the priory and riverside, before retracing your steps back to the car park (3h).

Bolton Priory

Founded by Augustinian canons in 1155, Bolton Priory enjoyed fluctuating fortunes until it fell victim to Henry VIII's order of the Dissolution of the Monasteries in 1539. Building work was still ongoing at the time, with the tower begun in 1520 left half-standing. The wild, haunting beauty of the ruins has subsequently been immortalised in paintings by Landseer and Turner, with a distorted image of the priory even resplendent on the front cover of The Cure's 1981 album *Faith*.

◄ Looking out from Bolton Priory

13

On Simon's Seat

Simon's Seat (485m) Walk time 3h40
Height gain 400m Distance 13km
OS Map Explorer OL2

A landmark for miles around, Simon's Seat dominates the mid-Wharfedale skyline: a classic, from the fine boulder summit to the return through idyllic, riverside woods.

Start at the parking area at the eastern end of Barden Bridge (GR052574). (Note: dogs are not permitted on the Devonshire Estate access land.) Walk up the road away from the bridge towards Appletreewick,

turning down to a riverside path after 250m. Follow the Dales Way beside the river through graceful meadows for 1.8km to a lane rising just beyond a farm building. Cross over a minor road and take the hard track opposite past a number of cottages, over Howgill Lane and up to a gate at the edge of the Devonshire Estate access land. Go through the gate and maintain the ascent zigzagging through woods. Arriving at open fell, shadow the wall bending around to the left (ignoring the track splitting right) and head northeast along a well-defined and perhaps overly cairned path to the cluster of boulders at the summit. Simple use of the hands brings you up to the trig point (GR078598) (1h30). Begin a gentle descent south along a very

clear path around Truckle Crags, bearing ESE (left) 250m on at the fork, to traverse across the head of a gill. Joining an easily graded stone track, continue downhill to the east of the gill for 1.25km to the edge of the access land. Continue down through dense woodland to a stile at the far edge of the trees (SP Waterfall Cottage) (2h30). Drop into the Valley of Desolation, pass Posforth Force (waterfall), cross the footbridge and climb briefly up the far bank to crest into open fields. Meet the track to the right and follow it down through parkland to the road. Turn right, then just before the bridge at the foot of the slope, veer left on to an improved path (SP To the Strid). After an initial stretch strolling along the level, a short, steep climb leads away from the water to a high, winding terrace through woodland, offering glimpses of the river below. Back in open country, follow an improved path down to the water by a castellated aqueduct. Cross two fields (the second of which doubles as a car park/picnic area in the summer) back to Barden Bridge (3h40).

Valley of Desolation

The Valley of Desolation acquired its evocative name in 1826 following a severe storm. At the time, the narrow valley was filled with rich oak woodland, until lightning, gale-force winds and flash floods swept through. The wonders of natural regeneration mean that, save for a few gnarled oaks and decaying shells, there is little trace of the devastation today; the eerie name, though, persists.

◄ The fine boulder top

15

Into Barguest's lair

Walk time 3h Height gain 180m
Distance 12km OS Map Explorer OL2

Venture into a mysterious gorge that may have inspired Sherlock Holmes' most famous case.

Start at the centre of Burnsall (privately owned riverside car park) (GR031610). Walk over elegant Burnsall Bridge and turn into the field (and sometime car park) on the right. Head northeast to join the river as it returns on a meander and follow it to Woodhouse Farm. Pass through the farmyard and continue on a track back to the water. Stick with the river now for 2km to a short stretch of sylvan wood rising above the water, one of the most beautiful settings in Wharfedale. Leaving the trees, take the path splitting left away from the river to the road. Turn left uphill and then right over a stile after 150m (SP Skyreholme). Gain height steadily along a green track to a hard track passing above the farm and climbing gently to the road. Turn right, following the road through the village to a fork by a bridge. Take the 'No Through Road' rising to the left. Some 250m on, approaching the entrance to Parcevall Hall, go through the gate on the left beside Skyreholme Beck. Follow a path that runs initially alongside (and never far from) the beck through a narrow valley to the foot of Troller's Gill (GR068618) (1h30). (If flooded take the small grassy ravine rising north on the other side of the last outcrop before the gill.) Walk into the narrow rock cleft, picking a way over and around the mix of large and loose rocks

◀ Troller's Gill awaits

along the bed. It is a haunting, remarkable place. After 200m the crags to the sides open out; after the third stile across the floor of the valley, cross the beck and a stile in the wall to the left. Crest the slope and traverse west to meet a broad green path, with yellow-tipped posts marking the way to the road (ignore the turning right to 'New Road'). Turn left down the road and then

right after 200m onto a hard track (SP Hartlington). Reaching the end of the third field take the right-hand fork to a walled track (SP Bridleway). Beyond farm buildings this narrows to a lovely old lane, dropping amidst glorious scenery down to a road. Cross straight over to a lane leading back to Woodhouse. Turn right before the farm to return to Burnsall (3h).

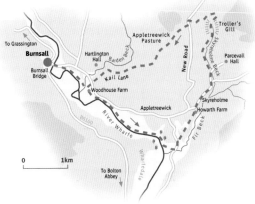

Elementary, my dear Watson

Sir Arthur Conan Doyle may well have based his *Hound of the Baskervilles* on a ferocious, spectral hound once said to have inhabited Troller's Gill. Local folklore has it that a terrifying wolf-like creature called Barguest, with 'rugged jaws', a 'wild bark' and 'fiendish glow' would kill men, leaving a distinctive mark on the chest of the victim. Conan Doyle had strong links with the Dales – his mother lived at Masongill, he was married near Ingleton and he was a regular visitor to the area. He almost certainly knew of the legend (which bears an uncanny similarity to his hound) and it is suggested that his novel was set on Dartmoor rather than in the Dales to deflect attention away from his mother.

Ghosts on the moor

Walk time 3h20 Height gain 260m
Distance 12km OS Map Explorer OL2

Gain an insight into the Dales' lead mining heritage along this moorland route, which boasts magnificent views to Barden Fell on the return.

Start in the centre of Hebden (just south of the B6265, close to the general store), where there is parking along the east side of the street (GR026631). Cross the B6265 and proceed directly up the road opposite for 850m to the tiny hamlet of Hole Bottom. Beyond the last house, go through the gate on the right; now follow a stone track alongside the beck for just over 1km to some ruined mine buildings. Some 150m on, cross to the opposite bank (stepping stones), crest the spoil heaps and keep with the track as it leads west up the valley side. Where it forks, go through the gateway to the right (SP Bridleway) to reach a much larger track after 100m ('Duke's New Road'). Turn right (NNE) and follow this for 700m across a wall and dammed beck to a further wall by ruined buildings (1h). Cross the stile, then almost immediately turn right off the track (as it bends sharply to the left) to meet the foot of the flue system running directly to the chimney (GR029665). Taking great care, as the flue is partially collapsed, follow it northeast for 500m to the magnificent, lonely chimney. Head north for 150m to tiny Coalgrovebeck Reservoir, then pick up the track 150m west. Turn uphill, taking the right-hand spur at the fork, then right again at the next fork. Walk east for 800m to a small reservoir to again turn right at a fork. Follow a beck southeast to a wall to shadow this

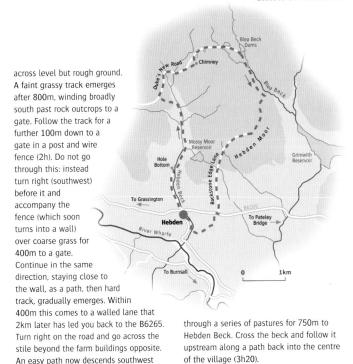

across level but rough ground. A faint grassy track emerges after 800m, winding broadly south past rock outcrops to a gate. Follow the track for a further 100m down to a gate in a post and wire fence (2h). Do not go through this: instead turn right (southwest) before it and accompany the fence (which soon turns into a wall) over coarse grass for 400m to a gate. Continue in the same direction, staying close to the wall, as a path, then hard track, gradually emerges. Within 400m this comes to a walled lane that 2km later has led you back to the B6265. Turn right on the road and go across the stile beyond the farm buildings opposite. An easy path now descends southwest through a series of pastures for 750m to Hebden Beck. Cross the beck and follow it upstream along a path back into the centre of the village (3h20).

Once an industry...

Evidence of lead mining here stretches back until at least the 16th century, but it was not until the early 19th century that the activity took on an industrial scale. Fuelled by the labour of hundreds of men and investment from the Duke of Devonshire, an elaborate network of dams, watercourses, winding machines and furnaces allowed the extraction and smelting of ore from deep shafts. The industry reached its peak between 1821 and 1861, when 170 men produced around 1000 tons of lead a year. The lasting icon of that period, the chimney (and the long flue leading up to it), was added in 1849. In a familiar story, increasingly awkward seams and cheap imports did for the industry, which was all but gone by 1880.

◄ The Grassington Moor chimney

Finding Mossdale Scar

Benfoot Brow (511m) Walk time 5h
Height gain 350m Distance 18km
OS Map Explorer OL2

An extended exploration of Grassington Moor to Mossdale Scar and Benfoot Brow, returning by the Dales Way across a plateau decorated with intriguing limestone flourishes.

Start at the YDNPA car park in Grassington (GR002637). Walk towards the centre of the village, turning right after 150m up the Main Street. By the Town Hall turn left along Chapel Street, then right up Bank Lane after 250m. At the head of the lane turn right (SP Bycliffe Rd) into a long narrow field. A clear, waymarked path ascends north through a succession of ancient pastures. After 1.5km, where the path splits beyond a wall stile, take the left fork. Pass a distinctive circular structure to

reach the derelict Bare House (1h). Round to the left of the buildings and head NNE to the corner of the next field. Cross the stile to the right, and continue north to a gate 100m on. Follow the short enclosed lane beyond back out onto the open moor. Continue north for a further 1km to reach Bycliffe Road. Turn right (northeast) down the track – after 1.5km Mossdale Scar is reached (GR016697) (2h). Some 500m on, the track, having crossed to the left of the beck at a ford, reaches a crossroads – turn left (northwest). After a short climb, the ground levels and the track fades out at a series of small spoil heaps. Drop down over Swarth Gill and continue west along an intermittent green path. A gentle ascent through heather for 1km leads to another set of workings by Benfoot Brow. Keep to the north of these to a signpost (SP Kettlewell) as the view over Wharfedale

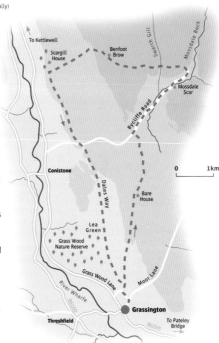

◄ Bare House (or 'Barras' as it is known locally)

opens out (GR000704). Continue 50m northwest to a ladder stile and descend for 600m in the same direction. Entering a second field, turn WSW directly down the slope along an initially faint green track that leads after 1.5km to the edge of the woods by Scargill House (3h15). Join the Dales Way path and head SSE along a wide, level terrace high above the valley floor. The route is clear and the going easy, with excellent views southwest and numerous points of interest (including an excellent lime kiln). After 2.75km, cross Bycliffe Road and Conistone Dib (4h). Press on in the same direction, over the plateau and Lea Green, along a well-defined route above Grass Wood to the head of Bank Lane (4km). Retrace your steps back through the village (5h).

The Mossdale Tragedy

The caverns beneath Mossdale Scar are notorious as the scene of the worst single accident in the history of British caving. On 24 June 1967, six young men negotiating the Grade V ('super severe') system were drowned when rain swelled Mossdale Beck, causing the caves to flood. The bodies were left where they were found until 1971, when members of the University of Leeds Caving Association interred them (with the agreement of the families) in a chamber of the system known as 'The Sanctuary'. The entrance to the cave system was sealed, but subsequently access has been gained and exploration continues on an unofficial basis.

Ancient lanes above Wharfedale

Walk time 5h Height gain 390m
Distance 18km OS Map Explorer OL2

Traversing ancient lanes (including the renowned Mastiles Lane), high pastures and valley meadows, this makes for an outstanding introduction to the variety of Wharfedale.

Start at the YDNPA car park in Grassington (GR002637). Head towards the centre of the village, turning right after 150m up the Main Street. By the Town Hall turn left along Chapel Street, then right up Bank Lane after 250m. At the head of the lane turn left (SP Dales Way) and follow a well-defined route through fields to the access land at Lea Green. Head northwest to shadow the wall above Bastow Wood – passing a fine limestone pavement on the way – for 1km to a ladder stile. Cross, turn right and drop down to the opposite side of a small, dry gorge (GR991662). Head west along the line of the gorge for 100m, then

crest the slope to the right, to pick up a path descending gently northwest for 1.25km into Conistone (1h15). At the road turn right, then left by the village square down the road to Kilnsey. Cross Conistone Bridge to reach a T-junction with the B6160. Turn left and then right after 75m (SP Cool Scar) up a hard track past farm buildings. Follow this for 500m, before swinging southwest up a short slope by a derelict building. Reaching Mastiles Lane (a wide stone track) turn uphill and walk WSW (SP Malham Tarn) for 2km to the highest point (425m), before making the short drop to Mastiles Gate (GR944661). Beyond the gate turn left, heading southeast for 750m to the end of Malham Moor Lane. Turn left along the road (SP Threshfield), entering a field on the right 50m after the next gate across the road. A green track contours around the slope then descends east for 1km to Height Laithe (3h15). Now cross

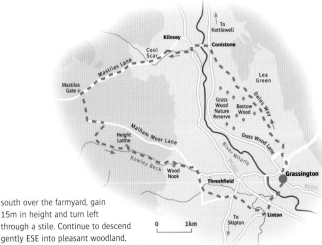

south over the farmyard, gain 15m in height and turn left through a stile. Continue to descend gently ESE into pleasant woodland, keeping to the left of a beck down to the campsite at Wood Nook. Follow the driveway past the main house and down to the public road. Turn right, pass straight over the crossroads and continue for a further 400m to turn into the pasture on the left by Grisedale Holiday Cottages. Head ESE across this and another field to join a minor road, turning left. Cross back over the B6160 (careful, it is a racetrack), taking the path opposite. Head ESE over three lush fields, cross the bridge over the defunct railway line (GR992629) and join the narrow walled lane to the right leading into Linton. In the village take the road bending to the left, bound for Grassington, over the brow and crossroads, bearing right at the bottom of the long hill. Turn down to the left before the first house, cross the River Wharfe and take the narrow walled path leading back up to the car park (5h).

Kilnsey Crag

Dominating the view on the descent into Conistone, Kilnsey Crag is not only a majestic example of glacial erosion but also one of the 'big three' climbing sites in Yorkshire (the others being Malham and Gordale). Some of the toughest sport climbing routes in England, notably the 9a-rated 'Northern Lights', are found here, together with many traditional routes. The prominent overhang responsible for this marks the height of the Ice Age glacier that scoured away the rock beneath. While sport climbing, with its fixed bolts and emphasis on gymnastic moves excites controversy it can be compelling to watch, let alone do.

◄ High pastures above Kilnsey

Malham, Littondale and Upper Wharfedale

No formal boundary divides Wharfedale, but just north of Kilnsey Crag, as Littondale splits away, the valley narrows and deepens into Upper Wharfedale. Something in the air changes here, too, and you feel yourself joining in these dales a ruggedly separate, resourceful and self-contained world. Tune into this mindset and this is a truly marvellous, timeless place. There is an intimacy and serenity that is easy to connect with and Littondale and Langstrothdale, in particular, are gems. But do not think that feral nature is tamed here; for all the sense of blustery romance in these hills, they are to be respected.

Here is all that the Dales should be – hymns to the harmony between man and nature. So, while the geographers will disagree, this is the heart of the Dales; a delight in other words.

The pleasures of Malham are different, but equal in their own way. Staggering under a deluge of visitors (pick your moment), the village does well to retain its integrity and to keep the tourist circus at arm's length. Why they come, and you should too, is the unrivalled geological interest, from the Cove to Watlowes and, of course, Gordale Scar. Rock lovers, enjoy.

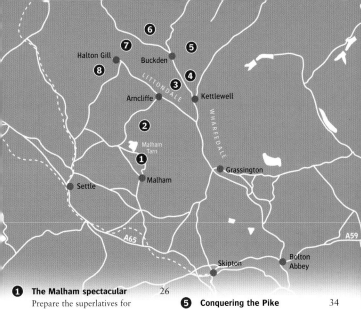

❶ The Malham spectacular   26
Prepare the superlatives for
Malham, home to some of the finest
rock scenery in Britain

❷ The Monk's Road to Littondale   28
The outward leg might just be the finest
route in the National Park. There can
hardly be a better destination, either

**❸ By the banks of the Wharfe
and the Skirfare**   30
Two rivers, two high crossings and
a revealing perspective on how dales
connect. Stamina needed!

❹ Great Whernside arena   32
A varied journey above Kettlewell
to a moody mountain and wonderful
views over Upper Wharfedale

❺ Conquering the Pike   34
If hefty Buckden Pike is an obvious
target, then the ascent by Walden
Road is a refreshing alternative

❻ Quiet times in Langstrothdale   36
With just a church, a pub, a river
and farms, Hubberholme is the
quintessential Dales hamlet

❼ The Horse's Head   38
Solitude is (almost) guaranteed on this
blustery, rounded moor. And, deep in
the Dales, the aptly-named Deepdale

❽ Along the spine of Pen-y-ghent   40
A traverse of this favourite mountain
leads to peaty Plover Hill and a descent
to the sleepy head of Littondale

◀ The infant River Wharfe, near Beckermonds, Langstrothdale

The Malham spectacular

Walk time 3h40 Height gain 320m
Distance 12.5km OS Map Explorer OL2

**Cove, Scar, Tarn... Malham and its
glories need little introduction, other
than to say there is no more spectacular
half-day in the Dales. Some simple
scrambling required.**

Start at the main car park in Malham
(GR900627). By the Buck Inn turn left on to
Cove Road (towards Town Head) and walk
out of the village, turning into the field on
the right (SP Malham Cove Fields NT) 100m
further on. Follow a family-friendly path to
the foot of the Cove then climb the
limestone staircase by the western edge of
the face. At the top, carefully pick a way
east across the superb limestone pavement,
making for a gap in the wall directly ahead.
Through this, traverse southeast up the field
and over the brow to the Malham Rakes
Road. Cross over to the path on the
opposite side (SP Gordale) and descend ESE
easily for 1km to Gordale Bridge (1h). At the
road turn left, then left again after 100m up
the broad path towards Gordale Scar. With
the cliffs closing in, round the head to the
right after 600m to reach the cleft of the
scar, with its dramatic rock formations and
waterfalls (GR915640). An initially off-
putting but straightforward scramble with
good holds leads past the main fall to a
very steep path rising to the left up to level
ground. Exiting the scar, head northwest

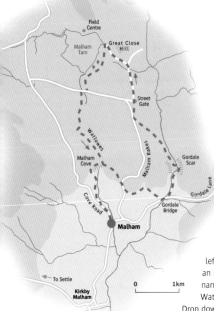

(2h). Go through the gateway and bear left behind the trees on a track that leads beneath the crags of Great Close Hill to the shore of Malham Tarn. Dip your toes in the water and then head south along a track running parallel to the tarn. Skirt around a small wood and bear right back to the shore, then down to the parking area. Turn right along the road, then left through the gate after 50m (SP Malham Cove). Ignore the Pennine Way path splitting left after 250m and head SSW along an initially broad but quickly narrowing way to the rocky head of Watlowes dry valley (GR892648) (3h). Drop down to the bottom of the valley and continue along its length as it sweeps through stunning, rocky terrain back to the limestone pavement on the top of the cove. Go west to reach the limestone staircase and retrace your earlier steps back into the village (3h40).

across a limestone-punctuated plateau for 1.5km to a wall stile, with a road beyond. Cross the stile and shadow the wall past Street Gate to join a hard track heading north for 750m to a cattle grid by a copse

Ward's Gordale Scar

Held in the collection of Tate Britain, *Gordale Scar* by James Ward (1769-1859) is considered one of the masterpieces of British landscape art. Painted during 1812-14 for local landowner Lord Ribblesdale, Ward's huge canvas, measuring 4.2m by 3.3m, captures the brooding majesty of the great gorge by subtly manipulating the perspective to emphasise the height and scale of the cliffs. In the foreground, a symbolic white bull guards the entrance to the scar. Hitherto, awestruck Romantic travellers had considered the scene too dramatic and sublime to be painted.

The Monk's Road to Littondale

Walk time 5h30 Height gain 430m
Distance 19km OS Map Explorer OL2

Forget the Gore-tex® for a moment and imagine yourself a medieval monk. They also walked this way, as did (much later) an inspired Charles Kingsley. You will be inspired, too.

Start at the Water Sinks parking area, 400m south of Malham Tarn (GR894657). Walk north to skirt around the eastern shore of the tarn. Approaching the woods by the field centre, turn northeast up the slope to the right. Crest the brow and drop down in the same direction to 100m before the farm buildings. Do not go down the farm track, instead turn up the short incline to the left (northwest), making for the gate and stile on the horizon (SP Arncliffe). At the top, shadow the wall to the right around a mound to a copse and derelict farmhouse (1h). Now head north beside the wall for a further 500m along a well-defined path, then contour northeast to walk beneath a series of small limestone escarpments. As a stunning ravine comes into view down to the left, the path begins to slowly descend, eventually narrowing to a thin terrace above crags (GR923708). A steep descent northwest brings you to a farm track leading into Arncliffe (2h15). Coming out by the pub, turn right and walk the length of the village green, then turn left on the road towards Litton. After 150m, bear right between the church and the old vicarage (by the stocks!) to reach a path beside the Skirfare. Marker posts lead an easy way through bucolic pastures for 2.25km (with a spectacular example of meander erosion en route) to an iron bridge over the river at the fringe of Hawkswick. Do not be tempted to cross and instead

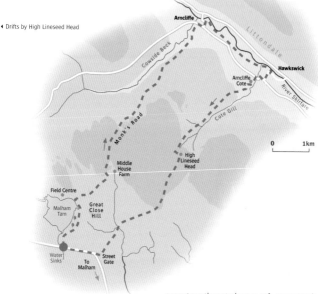

◄ Drifts by High Lineseed Head

walk up the narrow lane heading away from it. At the road turn right, then right again at the larger road (3h). Immediately after the bridge by Arncliffe Cote, turn left onto a farm track (SP Street Gate). Pass the farm and continue through a gate onto the open fell. An initial zigzag gives way to a gradual ascent southwest along a soft green track for 2.5km to the north of a gill. The track performs a sharp 'S-bend' at a steeper section just before the highest point (GR925680) (510m) (4h30), then descends southwest as easily as it rose for 3.5km to Street Gate. Turn right down the road to reach the parking area after 1km (5h30).

Charles Kingsley & Arncliffe

The limestone scenery of the Dales greatly inspired Charles Kingsley's enduring children's classic, *The Water Babies*, which was written in part at Bridge House, Arncliffe. Despite the youth of its intended audience, the novel addressed a number of potentially controversial themes at the time of its publication in 1863, including the working conditions of the poor (in this case chimney sweeps), the pollution of waterways and evolutionary theory.

By the banks of the Wharfe and the Skirfare

Firth Fell (607m) Walk time 6h30
Height gain 650m Distance 20km
OS Map Explorer OL30

Dale-hopping is a joy. Here, take in some of the best of both Littondale and Upper Wharfedale, and the tops in between.

Start at the YDNPA car park in Kettlewell (GR967722). Cross the bridge out of the village and turn down immediately to the right to pick up the Dales Way riverside path. This well-trodden route leads for 8km through meadows, walled lanes and woods to the roadbridge on Dubb's Lane by Buckden (2h). Turn left along the road towards Hubberholme to reach the entrance to Redmire Farm after 200m. From the farm lane, follow a stone track zigzagging up the slope to a gated sheepfold. Continue along the track out onto the open moor. After 200m turn off and ascend SSW up Firth Fell,

guided by intermittent blue-tipped marker posts. The gradient increases towards the top and in places the ground is rather wet (a problem the National Park has sought to combat by laying large paving stones). As the ground flattens out by the summit, cross through a gap in a tumbledown wall, keeping this and its more solid successor on your right as you cross the summit plateau (GR924749) (3h) and descend steadily into Littondale. With most of the descent complete and the village of Litton in sight you reach a rake to sweep you down to the west to the foot of Crystal Beck Ghyll. Follow the walled lane into the village (4h); at the road go right, then turn down a bridleway on the opposite side after 50m. Meeting the often dried-up River Skirfare, turn left to reach a ford after 100m. Cross, then 50m on turn into the field on the left by the signpost to Arncliffe. The route quickly leads back to the riverside

◄ Looking west above Littondale

and a short – and narrow – stretch where some care needs to be taken evading tree roots and slippery stones. Follow the way through Scoska Wood Nature Reserve and a succession of pastures to a walled lane leading to the edge of Arncliffe (5h). Cross the roadbridge and turn immediately left onto a bridleway. Shortly back on tarmac turn left, go over the bridge and cross the riverside meadow on the right. Climb the slope ahead into woods, over a final rock step requiring care and out onto the open fell. An obvious path now leads through limestone protrusions and heather more or less due east at an easy gradient up the fellside. Cross the wall at the top, which marks the boundary between the dales (GR952721), and descend in the same direction over springy grass towards Kettlewell. Some care is required at the scar above the village, which is breached at the suitably named 'Slit', a narrow rock step that requires the use of hands; from here drop back down to the bridge and into Kettlewell (6h30).

Limestone vs millstone grit

Littondale and Upper Wharfedale are composed of Great Scar limestone in the valleys, overlaid by Yoredale limestone on the higher ground with a cap of millstone grit on the very highest ground around the tops of Firth Fell, Buckden Pike and Great Whernside. The contrast between limestone and millstone terrain is quite distinct, with millstone making for a rather bleak, rounded landscape opposed to the fascinating sculptural detail of limestone. Farmers prefer limestone, too: loamy, freely draining soils are found over limestone, while acidic, peaty soils of little agricultural value generally occur over gritstone.

Great Whernside arena

Great Whernside (704m)
Walk time 4h Height gain 500m
Distance 13km OS Map Explorer OL30

An excellent loop around the Great Whernside bowl, with a marvellous descent and a stark introduction to the difference between limestone and millstone grit, an enduring story in these parts.

Start at the YDNPA car park in Kettlewell (GR967722). Cross the bridge by the Blue Bell Inn and turn right. Walk through the village, continuing up the Leyburn road by the General Store. After 150m, go straight on where the road bends sharply to the left. Pass cottages, go over a bridge and turn left onto a beckside track – a footpath by a subsidiary beck is marked for Hag Dike

after 150m. A good, broad path heads initially steeply, then more gently, up the green slope to the north of Dowber Gill to Hag Dike Scout Hostel, with the highest dedicated chapel in England. Go to the right of the building and up the loose stone slope behind. The building sits on the transition from limestone to millstone grit and the change in terrain is marked, springy grass giving way to heavy-going peat moorland. A series of yellow-tipped marker posts chart a northeastern way across a section of relatively level ground, before the gradient steepens to the eerie, boulder-scattered summit of Great Whernside (GR002738) (1h30). From the trig point head north across the top for 600m to Blackfell Crags, then descend, by a distinctive stone shelter, northwest to a wall. Where, 100m on, the

◄ Breaking light over Cam Pasture

path forks, turn NNW down an initially steep but easing slope. Again, this section can be boggy. Keep to the north of Tor Dyke to reach the Coverdale road. Cross the road and follow the grass track heading west. The track terminates at a gate after 600m. Go through it and keep with the path as it contours around the slope by the Dyke (3h). After 300m, you are joined by a green track from the right, leading down to Top Mere Gate. Just beyond, the track forks, take the left-hand

(downhill) branch signposted Kettlewell. Cross over Cam Head to reach Top Mere Road. This leads steadily down to the Leyburn road above Kettlewell. Continue down, retracing your steps back through the village (4h).

Tor Dyke

One of the Dales' most remarkable features is Tor Dyke. A huge linear earthwork, the dyke runs for around 2km across the valley head between Upper Wharfedale and Coverdale. Along most of its length the dyke has been formed by cutting a ditch up to 2m deep along the base of a limestone scar; then, where the scar finishes, the dyke continues as an earth rampart almost 2m in height. No one quite knows who built it or when, but theories include it marking the northeastern boundary of the Dark Age Kingdom of Craven and a native defence for holding back the Roman invasion.

Conquering the Pike

Buckden Pike (702m) Walk time 4h
Height gain 500m Distance 13km
OS Map Explorer OL30

The last outpost of Upper Wharfedale, rising high above the villages of Buckden and Starbotton, Buckden Pike makes for a rewarding ascent with a moving surprise.

Start at the YDNPA car park in Buckden (GR942773). Cross the B6160, cut down to the right of the village green to meet the Langstrothdale road; go over the bridge, then through the gate immediately on the left. Follow the easy riverside path SSE for 3.5km through woods, walled lanes and meadows to the bridge over the Wharfe by Starbotton (1h). Walk to the village, cross back over the B6160 and take the lane opposite. Wind north through the village to just beyond a small stone bridge at the far end. Turn up the steep track rising to the right, and prepare for a sharp climb. After 500m and a height gain of 100m, the gradient eases; at this point ignore the path beyond the gate to the left, and continue NNE along a rutted, soft green track (SP Walden Head). Rise to the west of the gill

into a wide, narrowing combe, over initially wet ground and then a stony path. Beyond the head of the beck, continue northeast up a steeper peaty section to levelling ground and a gate onto the open moor. Go through the gate and turn left, shadowing the wall for 1.4km, past the memorial cross and on to the summit (GR960787) (2h45). Cross over a ladder stile to the trig point, return south for 125m, and then drop southwest beyond a further stile to the disused leadmine. Pick a way between the spoil and ruins and contour south for 500m. Begin to descend gently SSW, initially beside a wall then following marker posts, to a short zigzag and a marker post beyond. Here, bear right (SP Buckden), dropping southwest beside the wall to a terraced incline sweeping NNW to above the village.

Cross Buckden Beck and follow the wall to the left over the brow and back to the car park (4h).

The memorial cross

The lonely memorial cross at the southern tip of Buckden Pike's summit plateau commemorates the five Polish airmen who died when an RAF Wellington Bomber crashed there on 30 January 1942. Overcoming a blizzard and broken ankle, the only survivor, Sgt Joe Fusniak, followed fox tracks in the snow down to the safety of the White Lion Inn, Cray, where he was taken in by the Parker family. In 1973, Sgt Fusniak organised the memorial to his fallen comrades with, in recognition of the animal that had saved his life, the statue of a fox's head set in the base.

◄ The memorial cross at sunset

Quiet times in Langstrothdale

Walk time 3h Height gain 140m
Distance 13km OS Map Explorer OL30

**A lazy day dedicated to the tranquillity
and peace of a sublime dale, with fine
pubs to detain you further in
Hubberholme and Cray.**

Start at the YDNPA car park in Buckden
(GR942773). Cross the B6160, cut down to
the right of the village green to meet the
Langstrothdale road; go over the bridge,
then through the gate immediately on the
right. Follow the riverside path for 1km to
rejoin the road, turning right. By the George
Inn, cross the bridge and head back along
the road on the far bank. Approaching
Stubbing Bridge 750m on, turn through the

gate on the left before the bridge (by the
NT sign). Now head upstream beside the
waterfalls and woods along Cray Gill.
Initially, the way is fairly level, until,
emerging from the trees, the path heads
away from the beck up the slope. After a
short climb, go through the gate beneath
the first farmhouse at Cray (1h). Turn up by
the far side of the house and go through
the gate on the left. An obvious path now
crosses a succession of high pastures for
2.5km to Scar House along an easy, level
terrace above the woods and scars at the
head of Wharfedale (broadly WSW).
Negotiate the limestone outcrops above
Scar House and continue along the terrace
through the gate above the barn. Continue

◀ Tranquility just east of Hubberholme

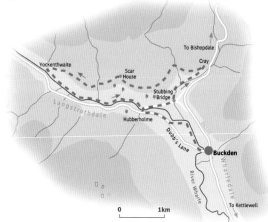

west for almost 2km, taking in the stunning views, to reach a stone track dropping down into the hamlet of Yockenthwaite (GR905790) (2h). Cross beneath the main farmhouse to pick up a path above a barn conversion that almost immediately drops down to the riverside.

Now follow the bank of the Wharfe ESE for 2.5km back towards Hubberholme. At the edge of the hamlet, shadow the perimeter wall of the church to a gate back onto the road. Cross the bridge and retrace the route back to Buckden (3h).

Hubberholme Church

Take the time to call in and view the charming interior of Hubberholme Church, which was declared to be 'very rough' by Pevsner, who pondered whether the style was 'essentially Norman, or essentially folk art'. And folk art it may well be, for the building, which dates primarily from the 12th century, possesses an honest simplicity and entirely human scale, from 'Mousey' Thompson's stalls (look for the signature mice) to the only surviving rood loft in the West Riding. Writer J B Priestley believed Hubberholme 'one of the smallest and pleasantest places in the world' to the extent he elected to stay – his ashes are buried in the churchyard.

The Horse's Head

Horse Head (605m) Walk time 4h20
Height gain 610m Distance 12km
OS Map Explorer OL30

Lovers of solitude and moorland need look no further than this criss-cross of a little-visited fell at the head of Littondale.

Start at the small parking area in Halton Gill (honesty box) (GR880764). Follow the Foxup road to the western edge of the village, turning up the hard track rising to the right. Walk with the track around a sharp bend to the right and then along a meandering route to the felltop. It is a steady climb, heading broadly northeast, with the track an infallible guide. Cross the wall at the top to the Langstrothdale side and drop down a stone path directly to the head of the ravine above Raisgill. Keep to the west of the ravine to complete a charming descent to the road. Turn left and cross the bridge over the Wharfe by Yockenthwaite (1h30). Go through the first gate on the left to join the Dales Way. Head through riverside meadows for 1km, before ascending gently in the direction of Deepdale. Just before the hamlet, pass over the beck, skirt the farmhouse and go down the lane to the bridge. Cross back over the river and take the track along the opposite bank for 2km (2h30). Reaching the final field before the plantation (across the river from Beckermonds), turn directly up the slope. After 100m or so, a faint path emerges between the plantation wall and the gully to the left. Ascend south across rough grass and potentially heavy ground

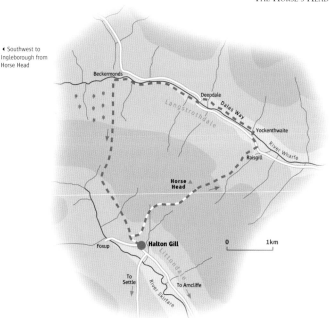

◄ Southwest to
Ingleborough from
Horse Head

up a steepening slope to a ladder stile
over the felltop wall (GR889776).
Continuing south, lose 70m, then traverse
southeast to a ladder stile. Continue in the
same direction down a gradually
steepening slope. Crossing another stile,

fine views over Littondale open up
beyond what is now quite a sharp descent.
Beyond a gate, meet the track
out of Halton Gill again by the sharp
bend. Retrace your steps back into the
village (4h20).

Walls and enclosures

Drystone walls are, perhaps, the singular motif of the Dales landscape. For all that, their
presence was not always so harmonious. The walls around small, irregular fields close to
settlements (west of Deepdale Bridge and east of Yockenthwaite, say) often date back to the
16th century, but most, especially those marching straight up and across hillsides, were built
during the period of 'the enclosures' from the late 17th century to around 1820, when large
parcels of common land fell into private ownership, never to return.

Along the spine of Pen-y-ghent

Pen-y-ghent (694m), **Plover Hill** (680m)
Walk time 5h30 Height gain 510m
Distance 17km OS Map Explorer OL2

Stalk what is arguably the Dales' best-loved hill along the length of its flank and then ascend by the classic ridge, before returning by the high-level route over Plover Hill.

Start at the small parking area in Halton Gill (honesty box) (GR880764). Walk south from the village, following Silverdale Road over the humpback bridge and up the eastern flank of Plover Hill to level ground. Immediately after the third cattle grid encountered, drop down into the field on the left. Descend briefly to pick up a narrow path contouring through bracken along the side of the gill. Pass beneath Pen-y-ghent House to meet the road again by the Giant's Grave. Now head southwest along the undulating road for 2.5km to Dale Head. Join the Pennine Way, turning right down a hard track past the farm and onto the open fell (2h). Continue along the track for 500m and then bear onto a path splitting right (SP Pen-y-ghent). Proceed north, joining a wall to the left after the next stile, to reach the foot of the summit ridge. This is a relatively steep climb with some loose rock, requiring the occasional use of the hands, but the route is well-worn and clear. After a gain of 130m the gradient eases and a short tramp (250m) NNE across gentle ground leads to the summit (GR838733). Cross the summit wall

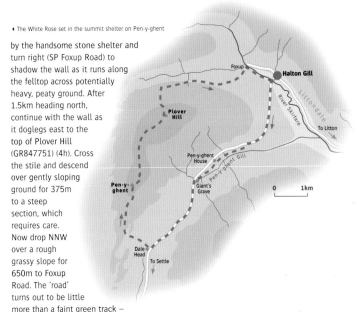

◄ The White Rose set in the summit shelter on Pen-y-ghent

by the handsome stone shelter and turn right (SP Foxup Road) to shadow the wall as it runs along the felltop across potentially heavy, peaty ground. After 1.5km heading north, continue with the wall as it doglegs east to the top of Plover Hill (GR847751) (4h). Cross the stile and descend over gently sloping ground for 375m to a steep section, which requires care. Now drop NNW over a rough grassy slope for 650m to Foxup Road. The 'road' turns out to be little more than a faint green track – turn to the right and follow it as it contours east for 2km, then descend to a gate by a blue-tipped marker post (SP Bridleway). Continue to another gate by a similar marker, and down to Foxup. At the road turn right, then right again after 50m onto the riverside path (SP Litton). Walk across lazy meadows for 900m to the humpback bridge crossed at the beginning. Retrace your steps back into Halton Gill (5h30).

Giant's Grave

The Bronze Age people venerated their dead, and relics signifying this are scattered about the Dales. Fully excavated in 1936, the Neolithic chambered cairn above Pen-y-ghent Gill, known as the Giant's Grave, is believed to be the oldest surviving above ground burial site in the Dales. Despite damage resulting from a prior attempt at excavation and the removal of stone for wall building, the remains of two stone flag built burial cists were discovered, containing fragments of human bone and teeth.

The Three Peaks and Ribblesdale

The first thing you notice about the southwest corner of the Dales is the sense of space. If some dales are enclosed and intimate, these roll on a grand scale beneath endless skies, dotted with notable features at almost every turn: the Dales' highest peak, longest waterfall, deepest cavern and so on. This is often called 'limestone country' and large parts of the uplands are dominated by that finest of rocks, bringing an angular, carved beauty to the landscape.

Naturally, the Three Peaks dominate the minds of walkers and while the reputation of Whernside may be exaggerated, Pen-y-ghent and Ingleborough are two of England's finest hills. That brings people and erosion, and if some of the solutions are as aesthetically unwelcome as the problem, they are nevertheless a necessity to be accepted. But for all the popularity of certain paths, there are also places to discover here that combine great beauty and solitude – Kingsdale and Crummackdale, for instance. Then there is the gritty flavour, too, hinted at in the wide, unforgiving moors, the ongoing quarrying and the dark past of the magnificent Settle-Carlisle Railway. And that leads to the second thing you notice: the remarkable variety in such a relatively small area.

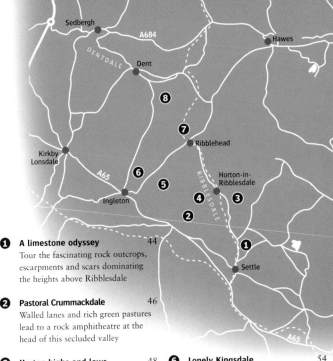

1 **A limestone odyssey**   44
Tour the fascinating rock outcrops, escarpments and scars dominating the heights above Ribblesdale

2 **Pastoral Crummackdale**   46
Walled lanes and rich green pastures lead to a rock amphitheatre at the head of this secluded valley

3 **Horton highs and lows**   48
A compact classic, from a direct ascent up the stepped 'nose' of Pen-y-ghent to a circle of precipitous Hull Pot

4 **A climb from the Sulber Nick**   50
Introduce a wilderness feel to the ascent of Ingleborough with an approach over the limestone plateau at Sulber

5 **The wild west**   52
The famed Crina Bottom route up Ingleborough begins an extended limestone round to Twistleton

6 **Lonely Kingsdale**   54
An expedition of contrasts, from the tranquil, elevated fields of Kingsdale to the wooded gorge of the River Doe

7 **Up and down the line**   56
After taking the Settle-Carlisle from Ribblehead to Dent, walk back and examine the achievement close up

8 **To Whernside from Deepdale**   58
Find the connoisseur's way up mighty Whernside, then return along the ancient Craven Wold

◂ The chapel of Chapel-le-Dale, in between Ingleton and Ribblehead

A limestone odyssey

Smearsett Scar (363m) Walk time 5h
Height gain 470m Distance 15km
OS Map Explorer OL2

**From the escarpment at Attermire Scar
to the handsome peak of Smearsett
Scar, this route is proof – if it were
needed – that the lower reach of
Ribblesdale is one of the finest
limestone landscapes in the Dales.**

Start from the marketplace in Settle
(by the TIC, limited parking – other car
parks nearby) (GR819636). Walk east up
Constitution Hill for 200m and then turn
up the walled lane climbing to the right
(SP Langcliffe). Arriving at an open field,
split from the main path and make the
short, steep pull directly up the slope.
Gaining level ground, drift ESE to shadow
a wall to the right. Pass to the south of
Warrendale Knotts and then turn north into

the cleft between it and the cliffs of
Attermire Scar (1h). Cross the stile and walk
north, directly along the foot of the
escarpment past Attermire and Victoria
Cave (GR837650). Reaching a track, turn
right. Some 100m on cross the stile to the
left, then turn north on the path branching
right after 100m. Drop down to the road;
turn right over the cattle grid and then left
down the lane 75m on (SP Stainforth).
Approaching a farmhouse after 800m, turn
down a walled lane to the left to another
whitewashed farmhouse. Walk through the
farmyard to the far gate, cross the stile
beyond and descend northwest. Entering
the woods by Stainforth Scar, descend a
rough, slippery limestone staircase to the
edge of the village. Walk into Stainforth,
cross the bridge by the Craven Heifer pub
and turn left to reach the B6480 (2h20).

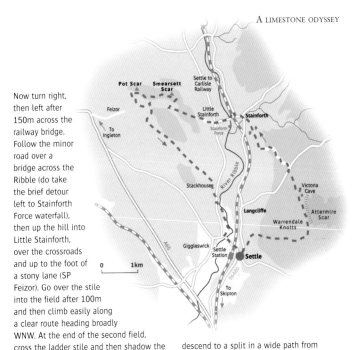

Now turn right, then left after 150m across the railway bridge. Follow the minor road over a bridge across the Ribble (do take the brief detour left to Stainforth Force waterfall), then up the hill into Little Stainforth, over the crossroads and up to the foot of a stony lane (SP Feizor). Go over the stile into the field after 100m and then climb easily along a clear route heading broadly WNW. At the end of the second field, cross the ladder stile and then shadow the wall to the right as it bends sharply north up to another stile on the flank of Smearsett Scar. Ascend the nose of the scar to the summit trig point (GR802678) (3h). Watching out for the crags to the south, pick a way west along the top of the ridge to the next peak, Pot Scar.

Continue in the same direction in descent, dropping to a stile to the south. Now return east, contouring through bracken, between the scar and a wall. As the wall ends, join the path rising from Feizor. After 250m, take the path branching south up the slope to the right. Crest and descend to a split in a wide path from the west. Take the left-hand fork (SP Stackhouse) and walk southeast for 1km to another split in the path, just after entering a field (4h). Walk through the gap in the wall to the right and descend southeast along a clear route for 1.25km to the edge of Stackhouse. Turn right down a rough lane (SP Stackhouse Lane) for 300m to a minor road. Turn right and then left into the field after 200m (SP Giggleswick). Follow a well-trodden route, high above the Ribble, past the school grounds and back to Settle. At the main road turn left to return to the marketplace (5h).

◀ Limestone outcrops above Ribblesdale

45

Pastoral Crummackdale

Walk time 3h20 Height gain 280m
Distance 11km OS Map Explorer OL2

Hidden Crummackdale's biggest secret is not its gorgeous blend of lush pastures, walled lanes and limestone cliffs, but how it has remained unspoilt for so long.

Start at the village green in the centre of Austwick (limited roadside parking, motorists consider using public transport from Settle) (GR767684). Walk towards the northeast end of the village, turning up the road rising left 50m past the school. Follow this up and out of the village, to where the ground levels off at a crossroads with a stony track. Turn right down the track, then left into the fields after 75m. Now head NNE across four undulating pastures for 1.25km to a stile, beyond which turn right and drop down to a beck. Cross the first bridge, then turn right by the second and go up the lane to the right for 50m, before taking the narrow walled lane on the left. This easy, level way winds beneath

increasingly dramatic rock scenery for 2km to its head by the foot of Moughton Scar (1h30). Go through the gate onto the open fell and continue northeast for 125m, then swing northwest to climb behind the initial lower outcrop to the top of the scar (GR783720).

Now pick a way carefully across the limestone pavement, following at a comfortable distance the line of the precipice to your left (initially west for 200m, then northwest for 750m). Reaching the end of the scar, a wall and stile ('Beggar's Stile') appear down to the left. Descend to the stile and proceed SSW through the fields for 1.25km (follow the intermittent yellow-tipped markers) to reach the track skirting Crummack Farm. Continue south on the farm track, which soon becomes a metalled road, for 1.75km (ignore the left-hand fork 800m after the farm) to reach a footpath rising to the right (SP Norber). Ascend WNW to the left of a wall, pass beneath a small escarpment and

continue for a further 250m to reach the edge of the Norber Erratics. Spare some time to explore the unusual formations, before easily descending SSW down to a walled lane. Turn left, then almost immediately right down the road back into Austwick (3h20).

Norber Erratics

The Norber Erratics are one of the most peculiar examples of glacial action in Northern England. Around 12,000 years ago, huge Silurian boulders were eroded from the head of Crummackdale, then carried by a glacier and deposited on the limestone roughly 1km south. Over millennia, the surrounding limestone surface has slowly been dissolved by wind and rain, but the limestone beneath the boulders has been protected by the rock above, so that now many of the boulders perch on small limestone plinths rising around 50cm above the ground.

47

Horton highs and lows

Pen-y-ghent (694m) Walk time 3h
Height gain 470m Distance 9km
OS Map Explorer OL2

**A half-day with almost everything
the Dales walker could hope for, from
the highs of Pen-y-ghent to the lows
of Hull Pot.**

Start at the small parking area by Horton
Bridge at the southern tip of Horton-in-
Ribblesdale (GR810720). Do not go over the
bridge, instead cross the main road and
proceed up the lane opposite. Pass the
village school and follow the lane into open
country. Reaching a barn on the left, around
600m on from the school, turn into the field
on the left (SP Pen-y-ghent Summit).
Climbing steadily ENE alongside the wall to
the left, the way soon introduces a terrific
view of the mountain ahead and a couple of
limestone outcrops to negotiate. An
improved path is reached, bringing you
quickly to the junction with the Pennine
Way beyond a double gate (1h). Now bear
north (left) to follow the summit ridge. It is
a relatively steep climb with some loose
rock, requiring the occasional use of the
hands, but the route is worn and clear. After
a gain of 130m the gradient eases and a
short tramp (250m) NNE across gentle
ground leads to the summit (GR838733).
Cross the summit wall by the handsome
stone shelter and descend southwest
(SP Pennine Way – Horton) along a well-
defined path, which turns after 200m to
head north towards a distinctive
escarpment. By the escarpment, break away
from the main path as it turns west,
continuing in the same direction, before
being guided by a wall to the north (right)

down to the northwest corner of the field. Cross over and continue northwest for 600m to beyond another wall. Turn south (left) to follow the sliver of ground between the wall and beck for 400m to the spectacular Hull Pot, the basin of which has been known to fill after severe rain (2h). Bear south along a track for 250m to the head of a walled lane. Follow this as it winds down through pastures for just over 2km back to Horton-in-Ribblesdale. Reaching the main road, turn left to return to Horton Bridge (3h).

The Three Peaks Walk

This ascent is traditionally the first stage of the Three Peaks Walk, arguably the most famous 'challenge walk' in Britain. Starting from the Pen-y-ghent Café in Horton-in-Ribblesdale, the aim is to complete the 39km round of Pen-y-ghent, Whernside and Ingleborough – taking in 1600m of ascent – and clock back into the café within 12 hours. Those who do so qualify for the right to purchase a 'Three Peaks of Yorkshire Club' badge and tie. Over the last 35 years it is conservatively estimated that more than 200,000 have completed it, making it not only the most famous, but also the most popular walk of its type in the country.

◀ Pen-y-ghent from above Brackenbottom

A climb from the Sulber Nick

Ingleborough (723m) Walk time 5h30
Height gain 565m Distance 18km
OS Map Explorer OL2

**A long, westwards approach to
Yorkshire's most famous mountain,
passing by the murky depths of
Gaping Gill.**

Start at the YDNPA car park in Horton-in-Ribblesdale (GR807726). Walk north across the footbridge over the Ribble and turn left at the road. At the sharp corner continue straight up to the station. Go through the gate to the left, cross the tracks and proceed broadly WNW along a clear path across undulating terrain. After 1km, the route settles on a gentle ascent through limestone outcrops to reach the level ground at Sulber Nick. Follow the dead-straight path towards the now visible

Ingleborough for a further 1km, to meet a junction with a N-S bridleway (1h). Bear SSW (SP Clapham) along the springy, green bridleway. It is easy walking for 2.5km (ignoring any branches splitting to the southeast) with only a very gradual descent to the wall above Clapham Bottoms. Leave the track and descend west to the bottom, aiming for the path climbing steadily up the far side. Follow this up and around to the northwest to a wall with ladder stiles, by which time Ingleborough is back in view (2h15). Continue in the same direction – do take the brief detour to the sheer edge of Gaping Gill after 300m – climbing up a steepening slope to the top of Little Ingleborough. Keeping above the eastern flank, continue north across the level top to the short final ascent up to the flat, featureless summit plateau, which can be a

disorientating place in mist. Strike WNW for 200m to the trig point (GR741745) (3h15). Now bear ENE to a cairn marking the line of descent. After an initial steep and rocky section, drop down east across rough grass to a path contouring along the southern flank of Simon Fell. Continue ESE along a well-defined stone path into a second field, where the rate of descent increases, then eases to a shooting hut by a wall to the left (4h15). Cross the next stile and keep on in the same direction (do not take the path to the right) to walk by limestone pavements back to the junction with the bridleway where earlier you had turned SSW. Retrace your steps back by the Sulber Nick to Horton-in-Ribblesdale (5h30).

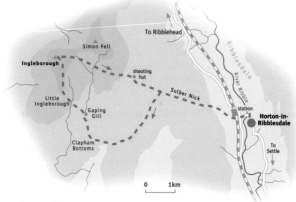

Going underground

As you look around the top of Gaping Gill, edging closer to the drop, bear in mind that it is almost 100m to the floor of the main chamber. In 1848, a certain M J Birkbeck descended halfway to what is now known as 'Birkbeck's Ledge', though it was not until 1895 that the first full descent was made, by the French caver Edouard Martel. Lowering himself by rope ladder, it took Martel 23 minutes to reach the floor (he was hauled back up again). When dry it is possible to climb out of the gill, though successful attempts are few and far between. In 1988, Paul Eastwood and Dave Hetherington made the first free ascent. For those contemplating the prospect, the climb is graded E3, 5c with eight pitches.

◀ Looking north from the summit of Ingleborough

The wild west

Ingleborough (723m) Walk time 6h
Height gain 715m Distance 18km
OS Map Explorer OL2

The scale and grandeur of these parts reach their finest expression in a superb, windswept horseshoe around the wild west of Ingleborough and Twistleton. Bring your navigation skills and prepare for a buffeting.

Start at the main car park in Ingleton, by the TIC (GR694730) (or, if you intend to return by Beezley Falls, the Waterfalls Trail car park, paying your fee). Walk into the centre of the village, following the road up the High Street. Beyond the last shop take the left-hand fork, then fork left again 200m on (SP Hawes). After the last house, take the stony track to the right (SP Ingleborough). The track soon becomes enclosed, rising steadily for 1.6km to the open fell at Crina Bottom. Drop onto the lower, grassy track and pass the farm, pressing on ENE up the steepening slope. It is a steady, albeit one-paced ascent, except for the three short, steep sections just beneath the top. The flat, featureless summit plateau can be disorientating in mist (2h). Walk ENE from the trig point (GR741745) to a steeply descending, narrowing ridge. Go through a swing gate (SP National Nature Reserve) and turn immediately left beside a beck (NNW), down a very steep and roughly stepped staircase. As the gradient eases, join an improved stone walkway, sweeping down over the next 1km to a wall. Cross into the 'Southerscales Nature Reserve' and follow a green track meandering broadly NNW through limestone outcrops. Leaving these behind, turn onto a path dropping down to the left past a whitewashed farmhouse and through fields to the road. Cross over to the minor road opposite and into Chapel-le-Dale (3h15). Pass the chapel itself and turn up the road to the right, taking the right-hand fork after a further 250m (SP Ellerbeck). Walk up between the trees along a track (note the sculpture) past Gill Head and out onto the open fell. Gently ascend northwest for a further 600m to the entrance to Ellerbeck Farm (GR730782). Head away from the farm, broadly WSW

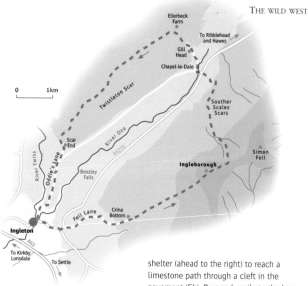

(SP Scar End), along an undulating, narrow and often vague path through rough grass. After around 1.5km, with an increasing incidence of limestone, note the wall to the right – there is no need to get close, but it is a reassuring guide as you weave between the outcrops. Aim for directly between a distinctive cairn (ahead to the left) and

shelter (ahead to the right) to reach a limestone path through a cleft in the pavement (5h). Descend easily to the lane above Scar End. (For Beezley Falls, follow the directions from Twistleton Hall, page 55.) Walk between the buildings and down the farm lane. Coming to a minor road, turn right and follow it into Ingleton. Reaching a T-junction, go left, cross the bridge and then turn right back to the main car park (6h).

Blood on the tracks

No one knows how many of the 6000 'navvies' who built the Settle-Carlisle Railway died in the process. Working conditions were harsh – this, we should remember, was one of the last major engineering works in the country undertaken with just manual labour – the weather fierce and the landscape isolated and awkward. Over 100 died building Ribblehead Viaduct, another 80 from smallpox following an outbreak at one of the moorland camps, with countless more falling victim to 'minor' accidents. Around 100 men are buried in the graveyard at Chapel-le-Dale; they, and the others, are commemorated in a tablet at the church, bestowed by their fellow workmen and the Midland Railway.

◂ 'Endless sky' and limestone pavement above Twistleton Scar

Lonely Kingsdale

Walk time 4h Height gain 300m
Distance 14km OS Map Explorer OL2

**As you stride along a high terrace, past
moody potholes, towards a sylvan wood
and renowned cave, you will wonder
why Kingsdale is so overlooked.**

Start at the waterfalls trail car park on
the western edge of Ingleton (GR693733).
Return to the road and take the path by
trees west of the entrance (SP Thornton
Hall). Cross the disused railway, walking
NNW to the northern corner of the third
field (just west of the Hall). Join the minor
road and continue steadily uphill for 1.4km.
Some 150m after levelling off, go through
the gate to the left (by a small hut) onto an
initially zigzagging green track rising gently
to level ground. Continue through a

gateway, beyond which the track gives way
to a sometimes rather vague path through
rough grass. Keep close to the slope rising
to the right and then walk up it along a
much more distinct path 400m on from the
gateway. Now follow this as it meanders
broadly north through limestone outcrops to
a stony lane (Turbary Road) (GR684767) (1h).
Turn right and contour northeast with the
lane, which soon enough morphs into a
green, occasionally rutted track running
along an open terrace. After 2km, take a
moment to look around the sheer top of
Rowten Pot (without getting too close!).
Beyond the next field, drop down by 20m
to contour along the top of Shout Scar,
crossing easily over a very low wall to
continue NNE to Yordas Wood. By the wall,
climb briefly to either a narrow stone stile or

◀ Beezley Falls

broken wooden fence, both of which allow easy access into the top of the wood (GR704791). Descend by the beck (which dries up halfway down) to the gloomy entrance of Yordas Cave at the foot of the gill (2h). Continue to the road and turn right. After 1km, cross the ladder stile to the left (SP Scar End). Walk southeast to Braida Garth Farm, rounding to the right of the first farm building. By the farmhouse, pick-up a path heading below the woods east across two pastures. Contour SSW across rough, tufty grass for 1.5km to the head of the Twistleton upland. Joining a smooth green bridleway, drop down to a lane leading to Twistleton Hall (3h). Keep this side of the building (SP Waterfall Walk) along an improved path to a minor road. Cross straight over and turn right beyond the farmhouse after 100m (SP Beezley Falls), joining the path to the falls along the River Doe. It is a winding, spectacular and sometimes busy conclusion to the walk. It's an easy route, too, leading back into Ingleton, where the return to the waterfalls walk car park is clearly signposted (4h).

The waterfalls trail

Parting with the waterfalls trail fee makes good sense – the paths beside the falls are worth it alone, but factor in the inclusion of parking and it should be a done deal (there is a pretty decent café, too). Anyway, the conclusion to the above walk requires you do, and if you are particularly keen on waterfalls you can walk the first half of the trail, too, beside the Twiss. All you need do from the head of the trail is turn left along the walled lane after Ravenray Bridge. This leads over the beck to the Kingsdale road; turn left and walk for 350m to the gate on the right. Quick getaway or waterfalls – it is your choice.

Up and down the line

Great Knoutberry Hill (672m)
Walk time 4h40 (including train journey)
Height gain 590m Distance 17km
OS Map Explorer OL2

**If the Dales we see today are a story of
the meeting between man and nature,
then here is its most extreme example.
Gauge the glorious moorland, and the
achievement of the builders and
engineers behind the Settle-Carlisle
Railway, both by rail and on foot.**

Start at Ribblehead Station where there is
a small car park for rail users (alternatively
there is plenty of off-road parking just north
of the junction of the B6255 and B6479)
(GR765789). Take the train north for 10
minutes, passing over three viaducts and
through Blea Moor Tunnel, alighting at Dent
Station. Walk to the access road and turn
uphill. After 1.8km of gradual ascent, turn
right onto a stone track contouring SSW
across the flank of Great Knoutberry Hill.
Just beyond a gate after 700m, turn up onto
the open fell, shadowing the fence to the

left. Note the very prominent cairn on the
horizon, a superb viewpoint over Dentdale.
It is a steady climb to the summit, over
rough grass with some wet patches
(GR788871) (1h20). Cross over the top,
keeping the wall to your left in descent.
Meeting the stone track from Arten Gill,
turn right. Just before a gate after 250m,
bear south alongside a wall to the right.
Keep with the wall over rough ground for
500m to an emerging path leading initially
south, then southwest through a small
depression to a wall. Cross over to the
remains of a walled lane, which quickly
reaches an improved stone track sweeping
down to the road. Turn right, descending
past Dent Head Viaduct to a whitewashed

cottage just after the boundary sign for Cowgill. Cross the bridge over the beck to the left and follow the path (SP Blea Moor) south to Dent Head Farm (3h). Walk through the farmyard and alongside the beck, meandering up to the edge of a conifer plantation (just above the entrance to the 2365m-long Blea Moor Tunnel). A partially improved path (wooden boards) leads SSW, across a forestry track and, after a short, steep pull, up to the edge of the moor (GR772834). Pass the air shaft, crest the slope and begin a long, gentle descent, passing by three notable spoil heaps and further air shafts. At the last of these the path levels out, then, after 1km, comes to a junction with a much larger path. Fork left onto an easy way shadowing the line past Blea Moor signalbox to the foot of the 396m-long Ribblehead Viaduct. Take time to admire the brooding majesty of the viaduct, then take the track leading southeast back to Ribblehead (4h40).

Under the axe

By 1984, years of under-investment had left the Settle-Carlisle Railway in bad shape; most of the stations had closed and only a few trains a day used it. Arguing that maintenance costs were disproportionately high, British Rail (BR) issued a closure notice. (Many now suggest BR deliberately shifted services elsewhere and exaggerated costs.) Outrage ensued: the pressure group Friends of the Settle-Carlisle, local authorities and rail enthusiasts campaigned to save the line. The resulting publicity and a growing realisation of its tourist potential saw passenger numbers more than quadruple between 1983 and 1989, when the government finally rejected BR's plan. Stations in the meantime had reopened (including Ribblehead and Dent, which were closed from 1970-86), while BR set to restoring properly the 21 viaducts and 14 tunnels along its length.

◄ Whernside looms over Blea Moor signalbox

To Whernside from Deepdale

Whernside (736m) Walk time 5h30
Height gain 600m Distance 16km
OS Map Explorer OL2

**Forget the more popular but tedious
ascent from Ribblehead, this is easily
the most interesting and varied – as
well as the quietest – way to the
highest point in Yorkshire.**

Start at the main car park on the western
edge of Dent (GR704870). Walk into the
centre of the village, forking right by the
George & Dragon pub. Follow the road out
of the village for 1.75km to a footpath on
the right (SP Outrake Foot) just beyond a
whitewashed cottage. The way leads for
1.5km through eleven pastures alongside

Deepdale Beck to a gate beside a gnarled
tree trunk. Go through the gate and drop
down to a bridge and across the beck. Head
for the top right-hand corner of the field
and pick up a path passing by Mire Garth to
reach Deepdale Head. Go straight through
the farmyard and up the slope (staying
close to the right-hand wall in the first
field) to reach the corner of the Dent-
Ingleton road by High Moss (1h45).
Continue up the road, going over the brow.
Almost immediately there is a green metal
gate on the left – go through this and begin
to ascend to the right of the fence. The
fence (it soon turns into a wall) makes for a
handy guide as it climbs directly up the
initially gentle and then steeper western

flank of Whernside. After gaining 175m of altitude the wall cuts away left, at which point contour south for 100m to a cairn, then resume the ascent east to the summit (GR738814). Cross the wall that runs the length of the summit ridge then turn north (left) onto a very prominent path. As you steadily descend the path morphs into an 'improved' stone pavement, joining a wall to the left running broadly east. Where the path turns away from the wall – to the right, roughly 1.5km off the summit – continue on with the wall for 200m over rough grass to meet with the Craven Way (3h30). Turn left (NNW) and follow this ancient route for 4km across the top of Great Wold and back down into Dentdale. There are stirring views to the north and west and the going is easy. Reaching Dyke Hall Road turn right (downhill), then upon reaching the T-junction with the Dentdale road, turn left, cross Mill Bridge and retrace your steps back into Dent (5h30).

When the Yorkshire Dales are not in Yorkshire

Whernside may be the highest point in Yorkshire, but geographically, only just. Most of this walk runs through Cumbria with the summit wall part of the current boundary between the two counties. In 1974, a national reorganisation of local government saw the scrapping of Yorkshire's three divisions, the Ridings (North, East and West; riding from the Old Norse *thrithjungr*, 'third part') that had existed for, it is claimed, 1124 years. Worse still, some western chunks of Yorkshire were absorbed into Lancashire with Deepdale, Dent and the area west subsumed into newly-formed Cumbria. To this day the controversy rumbles on, with a vocal group pressing for the reinstatement of the Ridings and Yorkshire's traditional boundaries. Be sure to wear your white rose on Yorkshire Day (1 August), the focal point of the campaign.

◀ The top of Yorkshire: the summit of Whernside

From the Howgills to Hawes

The folds and rounds of a distinctive cluster of hills rise in the northwest corner of the National Park – the Howgill Fells. An unfenced, smooth-sided massif, rich in possibilities, solid underfoot, with stunning vantage points and sparkles of interest, these are supremely liberating hills to walk. But beware the dull day – this particular landscape and mist make for a notoriously disorientating union.

Though it hardly diminishes their interest, the Howgills only really count within the Dales by historical association: they are at the margin of the area (probably beyond it) and physically very different, while the contemporary patterns of life in honest, no-nonsense Sedbergh feel the pull of Kendal (just ten miles west) far stronger than anything from the east.

Heading east from Sedbergh spread Dentdale, Garsdale and Mallerstang, thinly-populated, dozing valleys split by expansive, dreary and soggy tops (ignored here). Up high, the only relief is provided by the wonderful, conically-styled Wild Boar Fell, a reason to visit in itself. Of the valleys, Dentdale is the most engaging and easiest on the eye, while Dent itself might just be the prettiest village of the Dales, its cobble and whitewash allure falling just short of twee.

Further east still, above the broad arc of Wensleydale, a certain wistful, melancholy loneliness pervades the coarse grass and peat bogs of Great Shunner Fell and Dodd Fell, a spell even the sometimes populous Pennine Way fails to dispel. But, above all, find here the hidden delights of sublime Raydale, huddled around glinting Semer Water, the Dales' largest and finest natural lake.

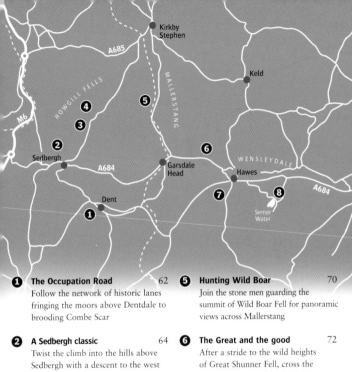

1 **The Occupation Road** 62
Follow the network of historic lanes fringing the moors above Dentdale to brooding Combe Scar

2 **A Sedbergh classic** 64
Twist the climb into the hills above Sedbergh with a descent to the west and an undulating return

3 **The rim of Cautley Crag** 66
Concentrated drama abounds on this short walk by the crashing waters of Cautley Spout and the dark cliffs of Cautley Crag

4 **The hills of the eastern Howgills** 68
'What goes up, must come down': and you will, again and again, around this enjoyably rugged traverse of some unfrequented tops

5 **Hunting Wild Boar** 70
Join the stone men guarding the summit of Wild Boar Fell for panoramic views across Mallerstang

6 **The Great and the good** 72
After a stride to the wild heights of Great Shunner Fell, cross the wooded incision of Cotterdale to the banks of the Ure

7 **The Sleddale round** 74
Superb routes in and out of Wensleydale sandwich a challenging round over some rough ground to two windswept fells

8 **Raydale surprises** 76
From tiny scattered hamlets to the charms of Semer Water, the traditional and unspoilt Raydale will delight

◄ Bram Rigg, Howgill Fells

The Occupation Road

Walk time 3h40 Height gain 250m
Distance 14km OS Map Explorer OL2

**If Dent is the pretty side of tranquil
Dentdale, then the Occupation Road
and Combe Scar is the gritty side.
Compare and contrast.**

Start at the main car park on the western
edge of Dent (GR704870). Walk into the
centre of the village, forking right by the
George & Dragon pub. Follow the road out
of the village for 1.5km to a footpath on the
right (SP Slack) just beyond Cage Farm: turn
off here and proceed up the field to emerge
at a lane. Take the path opposite, skirting
around the right of the buildings to come
out at the foot of a steep slope: climb south
up this and the next field. Beyond the wall
at the top of the second field, turn left by a

barn, then drop down to cross the beck on
your right. Continue your ascent south
through two further fields, before crossing
the top of a third. Emerging at a ladder stile
onto Nun House Outrake, turn right up the
slope. The track climbs steadily for 750m to
a junction with a green lane, known locally
as the Occupation Road (GR710845). Turn
right (northwest) here towards Keldishaw
and follow the lane for 4km across the
barren but beautiful South Lord's Land to its
junction with Barbondale Road. Turn right
onto the road; after 200m take the path on
the left (SP Underwood). Walk north across
the field to a ladder stile in the far corner.
Cross and keep close to the left-hand wall
for 100m before following the distinct path
as it contours northwards beneath the
eastern flank of Combe Scar.

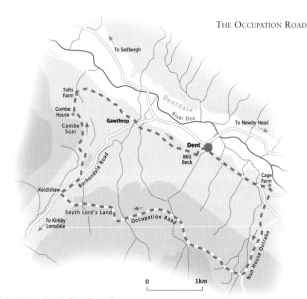

At the derelict and partially collapsed Combe House, drop down to the north to a tiny footbridge. Go through Tofts farmyard and descend the farm track to the road. Turn right, then bear right (after 300m) in the centre of tiny Gawthrop by the signpost to Dent. Follow the path through Gawthrop Hall farmyard, then across several pastures to Mill Beck. At the end of the farmyard, descend to the left to High Laning Farm and back to Dent (3h40).

The end of the road

Easily the most contentious issue facing the Yorkshire Dales surrounds the activities of 4x4s and trials bikes. The Dales are criss-crossed by a series of high, unsurfaced routes officially designated as 'byways open to all traffic' (BOATs). These were once major social, agricultural and trade arteries for the isolated communities of the area, built with the horse and cart in mind. Much to the chagrin of the off-road lobby, their use by 'recreational motor vehicles' is deemed an 'inappropriate activity' by the National Park, which has supported their exclusion from the most prominent routes on a 'temporary' basis since 2002, with some now closed permanently. A second blow was dealt to the 'mud pluggers' by the Natural Environment and Rural Communities Act of 2006, which extinguished the historic right that many off-roaders believed existed for them on more than 240km of bridleway and footpath in the National Park, including the length of the Occupation Road and Nun House Outrake.

◀ A helping hand along the Occupation Road

A Sedbergh classic

The Calf (676m), **Calders** (674m),
Arant Haw (605m), **Crook** (460m)
Walk time 5h30 Height gain 810m
Distance 14km OS Map Explorer OL19

**It is the classic ascent of the Howgills:
here, the high-level route from Sedbergh
to the Calf is twisted by a fine return
first along a narrow ridge and then
across the western flank of the hills.**

Start at Joss Lane car park in Sedbergh
(GR659921). Return to the entrance and
walk up the lane, following it around to the
right and up to the fell gate. Cross
diagonally over the field to the far corner
and then shadow Settlebeck Gill up to the
intake wall. Fork right, cross the gill and
begin to ascend northeast up the flank of
Crook. There is no path, but it is

straightforward to zigzag up through the
bracken along sheepruns. From the summit
cairn (GR664935), bear NNW across gently
ascending ground to the final, steepening
slope of Arant Haw. Aim for the summit
(GR662946) (1h40), ignoring the wide path
skirting the eastern flank. Now head
northeast along the top to pick up the
previously crossed path as it drops to the
narrow col at Rowantree Grains. Ascend
steeply north towards the top of Calders,
cutting back sharply NNE just beneath the
summit (GR670960). A wide, stony path
leads NNW over the broad, featureless top
of Bram Rigg Top to a small col and then up
to the Calf's summit trig point (GR667970)
(2h45). Drop back down to the small col
and join a path contouring southwest to the
superb Bram Rigg ridge. Descend steadily

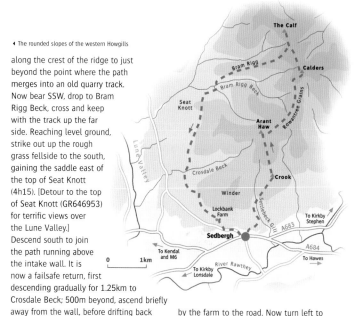

◀ The rounded slopes of the western Howgills

along the crest of the ridge to just beyond the point where the path merges into an old quarry track. Now bear SSW, drop to Bram Rigg Beck, cross and keep with the track up the far side. Reaching level ground, strike out up the rough grass fellside to the south, gaining the saddle east of the top of Seat Knott (4h15). [Detour to the top of Seat Knott (GR646953) for terrific views over the Lune Valley.] Descend south to join the path running above the intake wall. It is now a failsafe return, first descending gradually for 1.25km to Crosdale Beck; 500m beyond, ascend briefly away from the wall, before drifting back down to just above Lockbank Farm. Turn down through the gate, taking the left fork by the farm to the road. Now turn left to follow the road back into the centre of Sedbergh (5h30).

As seen on TV

Warhol's prediction of 15 minutes of fame came true for various members of the local community in 2005, when the people of Sedbergh starred in the BBC2 television series, *The Town That Wants a Twin*. The programme-makers followed the courtship between Sedbergh and four continental towns nominated as potential twins – delegations from each spent a week in Sedbergh, slipping (with varying degrees of success) into Dales life while promoting the attractions and benefits of their own towns. Zrece of Slovenia eventually won the popular vote by a landslide. Other notable film crew visits to the Dales include *All Creatures Great and Small* in the late '70s and '80s, in which Askrigg ('Darrowby') and the surrounding countryside played as large a part as any actor, and for the film *Calendar Girls*, in which Kettlewell donned the mask of 'Knapeley'.

The rim of Cautley Crag

Great Dummacks (663m) Walk time 2h30
Height gain 480m Distance 6km
OS Map Explorer OL19

**A short, steep and sweet excursion
in spectacular country, past one of
England's finest waterfalls on to the
rim of Cautley Crag.**

Start at the lay-by by the Cross Keys,
Cautley (GR698969). Cross the footbridge
over the River Rawthey and turn left on the
wide riverside path. After 500m (before the
footbridge) bear right into the Cautley Beck

valley. Follow a wide path WNW through
bracken across a glorious section of gently
undulating ground beneath the looming
crag, certainly the best way to approach
the spout ahead. Make the sharp climb up
the staircase beside the falls, which
cascade through a ravine for 175m. By the
top of the falls, contour left along a path,
crossing first Swere Gill and then Red Gill
Beck (1h15). Now ascend the grassy slope
to the south, following the line of the
precipitous crag. Naturally, increasingly
spectacular views develop across to
Yarlside and the eastern Howgills and, in

particular, into the amphitheatre below. The walking is easy with the proximity of the crags injecting a tingle of excitement. Reaching the crest after just over 1km, detour southwest for 150m to the summit of Great Dummacks (GR678963). Descend to the east down a long, relatively steep and grassy slope – broken by patches of bracken – to just above the intake wall (be sure to keep to the south of the cleft of Pickering Gill). Now pick up a path heading north to the footbridge over Cautley Beck. Cross and retrace your outward steps back to the starting point (2h30).

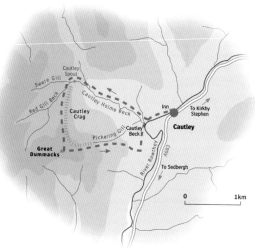

Sober Cautley

The handsome, whitewashed Cross Keys at Cautley is notable not only for its superb setting but also as one of the few temperance inns in Britain. The inn has been unlicensed since 1902 (though diners and guests are today welcome to bring their own alcohol) when Mrs Edith Bunney purchased it following the drowning in the Rawthey of the previous landlord as he tried to help a drunken customer from the riverbank. Mrs Bunney bequeathed the inn to the National Trust in 1949, stipulating that it remain 'dry'.

◄ The dark face of Cautley Crag

The hills of the eastern Howgills

Yarlside (639m), **Kensgriff** (574m),
Randygill Top (620m), **Green Bell** (605m),
Grere Fell (544m) Walk time 4h40
Height gain 740m Distance 12km
OS Map Explorer OL19

**The rolling heights of the eastern
Howgills are a perfect illustration of the
open character of these hills. Whether
up or down, this is a wonderful place to
spend a day.**

Start at the lay-by by the Cross Keys,
Cautley (GR698969). Cross the footbridge
over the River Rawthey and turn left on the
wide riverside path. After 500m (before the
footbridge) bear right into the Cautley Beck
valley. Follow a wide path WNW through
bracken across a glorious section of gently
undulating ground beneath looming Cautley
Crag. On the quickly steepening ground by

the lower reaches of Cautley Spout, take
the path splitting through bracken to the
right of the gill on the flank of Yarlside.
A steep climb now leads out to the col at
Bowderdale Head. Almost immediately bear
ENE up the rough grass slope to the right,
keeping to the right of the distinctive cleft.
Reaching the saddle of Yarlside, head NNW
to the summit (GR685985) (1h30). Walk in
the same direction for 250m to above a
very steep slope. Bear NNE directly down to
the col at the head of Little Randy Gill.
Continue NNE over the top of Kensgriff
(GR688992) to the small tarn at the foot of
Randygill Top. Ascend northwest up the
steady, easy-going grass slope to the
summit (GR687000) (2h30), a terrific
viewpoint. Follow the ridge northeast for
1.6km – over the subsidiary top of Spengill
Head – to the trig point on top of Green

◄ Yarlside from Cautley Beck

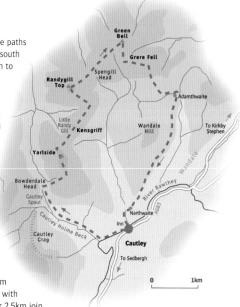

Bell (GR698010). Ignore the paths off the top and drop down south (east of Spen Gill) for 500m to the shoulder of Grere Fell. Walk east to the top (GR703005). Descend SSE over rough grass to a point just to the left of a modern agricultural building by the intake wall. Meeting a track, fork right to descend through a fenced section to the farm at Adamthwaite (3h40). Walk through the lower section of the farmyard (SP Narthwaite) to join a walled lane. This leads onto a generally good path along a high terrace (note the ruined farm and barns) above Wandale, with fine views to the east. After 2.5km join with a path from the right to a lane into Narthwaite. Turn right in the farmyard and then swing right along the track down to

Backside Beck. Cross over and keep with a lovely path for 500m to the footbridge back over the Rawthey (4h40).

Between a rock and a hard place

The Howgills have an identity all of their own, but the shadows of their much larger neighbours cast a sometimes confusing shadow. Sedbergh, for instance, lies within the Yorkshire Dales National Park, but is administered by South Lakeland District Council. Usually, for historical reasons, the Howgills are lumped for convenience with the Dales (here, say), but under the ground the rocks tell a different story. The Dent Fault, which runs for 32km from Kirkby Lonsdale to Kirkby Stephen, marks a clear division between the limestone scars of the Dales and the Silurian rock of the Lake District. And, in that respect, the Howgills most certainly look west.

Hunting Wild Boar

Wild Boar Fell (708m), **Swarth Fell** (681m) Walk time 5h Height gain 605m Distance 15km OS Map Explorer OL19

Ah, the freedom of the hills... leave sleepy Mallerstang Common for the fine summit of Wild Boar Fell and a chance to maverick across some open country.

Start at a small parking area just south of The Thrang, Mallerstang (GR783005). Go through the gate on the western side of the road, marked Deepgill. Follow the track over the bridge, then walk south from the corner of the wall. Cross four fields to a stone lane. Turn uphill, walk to the left of the farm and join a rising track. Pass beneath a railway bridge and then zigzag back to the right along a track. Just beyond a gateway, turn to climb directly up the slope. Note the fine, conical appearance of the summit from

this direction. As the gradient steepens after a flatter section, the path fades – continue west up the hill to gain the ridge close to a wall to the right. Now head SSW, initially along gently rising ground, then to the right of the developing crags at The Nab. Reaching the summit plateau (GR762990) (1h30), ignore the path branching WSW to the trig point and instead follow the line of the top of the eastern cliffs to the group of seven stone men (GR761984). Continue along the top of the crags for a further 250m and then bear west to the southern edge of the plateau above The Band. (Do not be tempted to drop down to Aisgill Head – it is wet.) Continue around the edge to meet a fence, shadowing it down to the col. Walk to the west of the tarn and join a

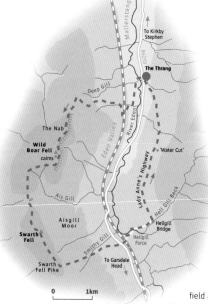

fence down for 100m and then strike out ENE, descending across rough but giving grass. There is no path and the crossing of Smithy Gill may be wet, but the going is relatively easy. Be sure to aim for the ground right of the distinctive cleft in Smithy Gill, from where vehicle tracks may be picked up leading down to the road just south of Aisgill Moor Cottages. Cross the road and walk up the farm track opposite. At the fork turn right, pass Hellgill Force and keep with the track to its end beyond the farm. Walk up the field ahead to a wide, green lane on the other side of the top wall. Turn left and follow the gently rising Lady Anne's Highway for 1.75km to the gorgeous sculpture *Water Cut* by Mary Bourne at the high point (440m) (GR785985). It is now an easy, failsafe descent along a stone track to the road and parking area (5h).

wall to the right climbing towards the flat top of Swarth Fell. The rocky summit is located 130m east of the wall beyond a small tarn (GR755966) (2h45). Now walk SSE across level ground, over the dip and on to the top of Swarth Fell Pike. Follow the

Ticking off

I suppose Sir Hugh Munro (1856-1919) is to blame. His initial catalogue of Scottish hills over 3000ft has inspired an apparently ever-growing list of arcane British hill categories. In England, the so-inclined can dutifully tick off the 'Nuttalls', 'Hewitts', 'Wainwrights' and 'Marilyns'. With two equal points of 708m – one at the trig point and one just northwest of the stone men – Wild Boar Fell (a Nuttall, Hewitt and Marilyn) presents the unusual problem that the completist must presumably visit both summits. For those who seek an escape in the hills from the imperative to list and order, 'peakbagging' must remain a mystery.

The Great and the good

Great Shunner Fell (716m) Walk time 6h
Height gain 575m Distance 18km
OS Map Explorer OL19

Great Shunner Fell has its detractors, but few can argue with the beauty of the valleys at its feet. Take them in, along with the highest point between Wensleydale and Swaledale – a case of the great and the good, if you like.

Start at the roadside parking area in Appersett (GR858906). [Please note that other than on public rights of way, dogs are not permitted on the open access land between Crag End Beacon (GR843955) and Cotterdale Woods (GR836948).] Walk west over the bridge and follow the A684 for 300m, over a humpback bridge to a stile at the junction with the Hardraw road (SP Bluebell Hill). Walk broadly north along a marked path across four fields to a wide, walled lane – turn uphill. Coming to open fell after 250m, take the left fork in the track (SP Pennine Way). Keep with the track for 1.5km to the gate at Hearne Top, beyond

which press on directly up the slope, ignoring the track as it contours northwest. The gradient is always easy, with considerable sections of level ground; at the first of these, the way settles on a steady north bearing for 2.5km to the final summit slope. With height the going becomes progressively boggier, though subtle stone improvements to the path have done much to alleviate this. From the last ascent before the top, the path moves northeast to reach the solid summit shelter (GR848972) (2h30). Retrace your steps for just under 2km to a large cairn at the top of a short descent, Crag End Beacon (GR843955). Now break off the path and descend WSW for 600m across rough grass to an overgrown green track contouring above the top of the conifer plantation. Walk south to a junction with a track dropping into the woods, then zigzag down this (it is well signed) until, with the end of the plantation in sight, a signpost (Bridleway) indicates a path cutting to the right by a small beck. Emerging, cross the river at a footbridge (3h40), and follow the

◄ Great Shunner Fell from the
pastures south of Hawes

track beside the water south into
the village. After 300m, as the road
bends right, break left to follow the
right-hand bank of the beck into
fields (SP Public Footpath). Take
the bridge over the beck and
rise (over a rather wet section)
directly to the road. Cross
over and continue up
through reedy grass (SP
Thwaite Bridge). Crest
the ridge and descend
southwest to a path
through a small wood
leading out to the
bridge. Cross the A684
and follow the path climbing
the short slope opposite. After
300m go through the gate to the
left and descend across the gill
to Mossdale Head (5h). Walk between
the byre and farmhouse to reach a path
across a series of riverside pastures. After
1km a stone track is reached – follow this
along Hollin Bank past Birkrigg Farm.
As the track curves towards the road,
continue in the same direction as before.

(SP Appersett). Cross the field to a beck in
the far right corner and climb the wooded
bank beyond. Now walk east above the trees
before gradually dropping back to the
riverside and returning to Appersett (6h).

A long green trail

At the summit of Great Shunner Fell, the Pennine Way reaches its highest point in the Dales.
Journalist Tom Stephenson is regarded as the inspiration behind Britain's first long-distance
path, having proposed something similar in an article 'Wanted: A Long Green Trail' in
1935. After the war, Stephenson became the first full-time secretary of the Ramblers
Association, cajoling the Government to support the idea. Eventually, in 1951, the Pennine
Way was designated, with the final section opening at a ceremony on Malham Moor in
April 1965 attended by over 2000 walkers, Tom Stephenson included.

The Sleddale round

Dodd Fell (668m), **Drumaldrace** (614m)
Walk time 5h Height gain 495m
Distance 16km OS Map Explorer OL30

**Hefty, rounded hills dominate the
Wensleydale skyline – strike out over
two rough moors and the fine tracks in
between, including High Cam Road,
which was built by the Romans, on a
round above Sleddale.**

Start at Gayle Lane car park in Hawes
(GR870897). Return to the road and walk
left past the creamery into Gayle. Just
before the bridge turn down the lane to the
right. Follow this to its conclusion at a
T-junction; turn right, then left into the field
after 20m. Following the Pennine Way signs
bear right after 100m, right again at the
lane, then left after 20m on to a surfaced
farm lane. At the foot of the driveway to the
farm, go through the gate on the left.
Ascend steadily to the head of the field.

Beyond the wall the going is a little rough
(and wet), but the route southwest is easy
enough to follow. After 1km, a lovely green
path emerges, soon joining a broken down
wall to reach a stone track. Follow the track
along level ground into a walled section.
Around 500m after leaving this, strike out
up the fellside to the south. There is no path
to ease the way and it can be hard going
over rough ground, with plenty of peat hags
and wet sections to keep your feet nimble.
Keep bearing south for 1.2km to the summit
trig point (GR840845) (2h15). Now descend
southeast across equally awkward terrain,
making a beeline for the wall. Follow this
east – around two corners – to Cam High
Road (a Roman Road). Turn left and follow
this to the junction with the Langstrothdale
road. Continue in the same direction with
excellent views back to Dodd Fell and over
Sleddale, before moving on to the track
splitting right after 700m, just as the road

begins to descend sharply. A wall to the left encloses the track after another 700m. Some 100m after this ends, break left up the slope to gain the 25m to the summit cairn of Drumaldrace (GR873867) (3h45). Return to the track and continue ENE for 800m to a stile on the left, just as the lane again becomes enclosed. After an undulating section, descend with a winding, recessed stone path for 500m before crossing over into the field to the left. Drop down to the northwest through a succession of pastures along a faint path – the gradient has something of a stepped profile along here, with two steep sections sandwiched between much easier terrain. After the second steep section, cross the next field (passing to the right of a barn) before bearing WNW to return over four fields to the edge of Gayle. At the road turn left, cross the bridge and then swing right to return to the car park (5h).

Say 'cheese'

The proprietor of Monty Python's Cheese Shop, Mr Wensleydale, famously had no cheese to sell, though you should have no problem securing Wensleydale's most famous product in Hawes, with the creamery itself the obvious starting point. It was not always thus: in 1992, then owners Dairy Crest closed the facility, ending production in the dale and transferring it to Lancashire. Six months later, a management buyout rescued the creamery and production resumed. The big break came in 1995, with the revelation in the film *A Close Shave* that Wensleydale was star Wallace's favourite cheese. Demand subsequently rocketed, securing the future of the creamery, with Aardman Animations even licensing Wallace & Gromit to appear on a specially-packaged variety.

◄ Dodd Fell and Cam High Road from Drumaldrace

Raydale surprises

Walk time 4h Height gain 300m
Distance 13.5km OS Map Explorer OL30

The largest natural lake in Yorkshire, England's shortest river and an evocative ruined chapel – gorgeous Raydale is full of surprises.

Start in the centre of Bainbridge (on-street parking by the village green) (GR933902). Walk south, continuing onto a back street (SP River Bain) as the A684 bends left for the bridge. After 25m fork right (SP Semer Water) and walk to the head of the lane and into a field. Keep initially to the wall on the right and ascend easily to undulating ground and the pony centre at Gill Edge. Turn right at the farm track, then right again at the road. At the second sharp bend, head onto the track breaking left (SP Beggarman's Road) – Cam High Road. Built by the Romans, the route is ruler straight for 2.25km to a crossroads (GR905883). Turn up the road, crest the ridge into Raydale and descend for 500m to a sharp left bend (1h30). Cross the stile to the right (SP Marsett Lane). After three further stiles in quick succession, descend south through fields to a track by agricultural buildings. Continue to the road, turn right and walk the 1.5km into Marsett. Immediately after the bridge, turn left to join a loose stone track running beside Marsett Beck. Soon enough, this moves away from the water as a walled lane, then opens out. Cross two metal footbridges,

veering left after the second. At the foot of the slope, cross over the wall to the left by a barn (GR9111859) and join a narrow path contouring northeast. Take a look at the ruined Stalling Busk Old Church after 600m, with the shore of Semer Water reached after a further 600m. Continue through the fields to Low Blean. Turn left along the road and then take the path beside the River Bain just before Semer Water Bridge (SP Bainbridge) (3h). After a sharp meander, follow the path away from the water, rising to crest Bracken Hill (GR932890). Descend north, shadowing the

line of the minor road on the other side of the wall after 600m. Reaching the A684, turn left and cross the bridge back into Bainbridge (4h).

A Raydale ruin

When the time comes, there could hardly be a more idyllic setting in which to be interred than the grounds by Stalling Busk Old Church, just to the southwest of Semer Water. The church is now a ruin, but was in use as little as 100 years ago. It was then in a bad state of repair, its fate being sealed by the building of a new parish church in 1908. The roof and fittings were soon stripped, leaving only a shell. Work in 1981 and more recently with the support of the Millennium Commission has helped to consolidate the ruin – some of the stonework dates back to 1602. The parish of Stalling Busk covers all of Raydale and it is believed that around 750 people lie buried in the old churchyard.

Lower Wensleydale and Swaledale

At times in Wensleydale it feels as if the flavours of the world outside the Dales have long since dissipated and dissolved. In Thornton Rust or Castle Bolton a dog could just about sleep in the middle of the road and get away with it. Still ostensibly agricultural, with the necessities of tourism more veiled than in the south, life moves to a relaxed rhythm here, and in that it finds a mirror in the landscape. The generally languid River Ure – save for the entertaining turmoil at Aysgarth Falls – weaves through lush pastures, bracketed across a wide valley floor by gently-graded, reclining fellsides, cut occasionally by small escarpments (as at Penhill). Hardly dramatic, the walking here is comforting and pleasing, replete with

historical interest. This is a gentle place, at ease with itself.

Swaledale is more contradictory. On one hand, this is the most beautiful of the major dales: a sinuous, enclosed valley with elaborate field patterns and rustic barns, a vivid river and exuberant waterfalls. On the other, the Dales' most concentrated industrial legacy echoes a bleak story of hardship, through the hushes, levels, spoil heaps and lead mining ruins scattered across the moors. And, along with neighbour Arkengarthdale, Swaledale feels noticeably remote (a mixed blessing), all the more so on the journey west to its head and the beckoning Pennine wilderness beyond Keld.

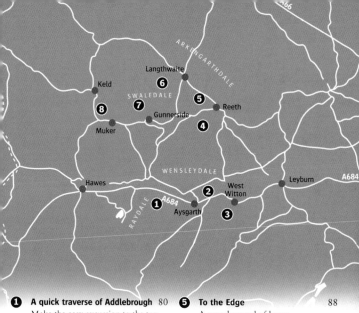

1 **A quick traverse of Addlebrough** 80
Make the easy excursion to the top of this small but interesting hill, an eyrie above Wensleydale

2 **Bolton Castle wanderer** 82
Seek out the magical rolling pastures leading from Aysgarth Falls to the imposing stone walls of Bolton Castle

3 **Knights and Scars** 84
Crags, meadows and deep historical connections combine in this picturesque ascent from West Witton

4 **High on Harker Hill** 86
Spectacular views and Iron Age earthworks vie for your interest, before a return beside the Swale

5 **To the Edge** 88
A superb round of lower Arkengarthdale, from heathery Calver Hill to the high edge at Fremington

6 **Arkengarthdale explorations** 90
An extended moorland excursion, mainly on miners' tracks, to lonely Great Pinseat

7 **Two sides of Swaledale** 92
Here, the swollen lunar spoil of Gunnerside Gill; there, the stunning pastoral beauty of Ivelet Side

8 **Beyond Kisdon** 94
Venture over the smooth slopes of Kisdon to the sparse, untamed moorland beyond

◀ Reeth village green and Fremington Edge

A quick traverse of Addlebrough

Addlebrough (480m) Walk time 2h15
Height gain 230m Distance 7.5km
OS Map Explorer OL30

When time is tight, this entertaining traverse of the small but characterful Addlebrough will fit the bill perfectly.

Start at the small car park in the centre of Thornton Rust (space for about six cars, otherwise some on-street parking by the village green) (GR972888). Return to the road and turn left. Walk for 1.25 km to a ladder stile on the left (SP Permissive Path, Addlebrough) and cross. At the head of the second field go over the stile to the right and continue straight up, initially alongside a beck. As the climb eases (after a further 500m) bear southwest, shadowing the wall to the left at a reasonable distance across rough, tufty grass (there is a faint and sometimes vague path). Beyond a further ladder stile, a short, steep ascent ends suddenly at the summit plateau (1h). Bear northwest away from the current cairn (GR947880) to the site of the original, marked by a number of distinctive stones, close to the northern lip of the plateau. From here walk the short distance west to the top of the crags, which offers a superb panorama over Raydale and Wensleydale. Now cross over the low fence immediately to the south – where the wall is collapsed at the end – just above one of the few breaks in the southwestern escarpment.

It is not difficult to pick the short way SSE down to a ruined settlement and from there to contour in the same direction to the bridleway from Carpley Green. There follows an easy, uneventful tramp (ENE, turning northeast) over a green, springy path for 2km to the edge of the access land. Descend through one more field to reach the head of a walled lane, leading 1km later directly back to the car park (2h15).

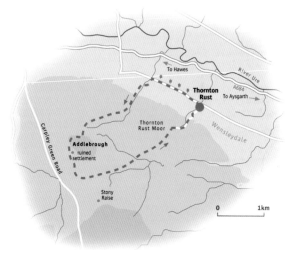

Ancient Addlebrough

There are numerous points of prehistoric interest on Addlebrough, not least the site of the original summit cairn. Only a circle of foundation stones remain, but most are cup-marked and are believed to date from the Bronze Age, while an old Yorkshire rhyme asserts: 'Druid, Roman, Scandinavia, Stone raise on Addleboro'. While there was certainly a Roman summer fort at the top of the hill, it is also believed that there was a much older presence there, with Ella Pontefract (*Wensleydale*, 1936) speculating that the site 'may have been the burial-place of Authulf, a British chief from whom the hill gets its name'. (See also the remains of the huge cairn at Stony Raise, 500m SSE of the point at which the Carpley Green bridleway is joined.)

◄ Addlebrough from the northeast

Bolton castle wanderer

Walk time 2h40 Height gain 190m
Distance 11km OS Map Explorer OL30

Whether your goal is Castle Bolton or Bolton Castle, this walk will reward with an enticing pastoral journey through the gentle folds of Wensleydale.

Start at the YDNPA car park at Aysgarth Falls (GR011887). Walk east to the road and cross, following the signs for the Lower Falls. A broad stone path leads through the woods for 700m to a cul-de-sac viewing platform by Lower Force. Return to the path and continue in the same direction as before to a stile. Walk up the slope to join a path heading northeast through fields to Hollins Farm; cross the farmyard, taking the track beyond for 100m to a gate on the

right. Despite the odd twist and turn, the direction is now broadly northeast all the way to the castle. First, cross three meadows to High Thoresby. To the right of the farm, take an old stone track past a barn, then 50m on turn into the field on the right and continue as before. Reaching another track after 500m, turn left up to the road. Turn right and keep with the road for 400m to a sharp bend. Take the path on the left (SP Castle Bolton) across two fields to the dismantled railway line. Walk to the rear of the cottages and join the lane rising up to the road. Continue around the castle, joining a lane heading west by the car park (GR033918). Go through the gate out onto the open fell (1h20). Follow the undulating stone track for 2km, past a knot of modern

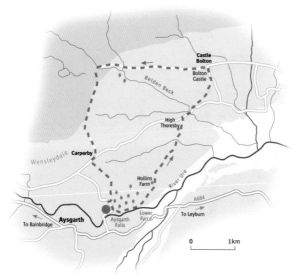

farm buildings to a dip above woods. Beyond, marker posts indicate the green path as it runs through bracken. Just after a gate, fork left (SP Carperby), descending beside a wall to a surfaced lane. Coming to Carperby village green, fork right and right

again at the road. Take the path opposite The Wheatsheaf pub (SP Aysgarth) to go over Low Lane and across a string of small ancient pastures, bearing south into coppiced woods. At the road turn left, pass beneath the bridge and then turn right back to the YDNPA car park (2h40).

Bolton Castle

One of the best-preserved medieval castles in Britain, the mightily impressive Bolton Castle has remained in the same family since it was built at the end of the 14th century by Sir Richard Le Scrope. A classic example of a fortress palace, it blends what would have been opulent luxury for the time with resolute defensive mechanisms, from a double portcullis to fireloops and walls nine feet thick in places. The fiercely royalist Scropes put these to good use during the Civil War when the castle held out for months before being taken by the roundheads in 1645. Much of the damage that resulted in the ruins visible today can be traced back to then.

◂ Bolton Castle

Knights and Scars

Walk time 3h40 Height gain 380m
Distance 12km OS Map Explorer OL30

Fine moorland scars and a history rich in associations with the Knights Templar ensure that both the eye and mind remain fully engaged on this colourful jaunt across the flank of Penhill.

Start at the lay-by on the A684 just east of West Witton, where there is space for around a dozen cars (GR064884). Walk into the village and turn left up the road to Carlton and Melmerby. After 200m take the narrow pathway on the right (SP Kagram) to fields. Entering the third field, turn up to the left for a short climb through the woods. Emerging, walk to the left of a young plantation (SP Watery Lane). Cross the green lane at the end of the field and ascend directly up the slope, across the lane beyond (High Lane) and up a section

with a stepped profile to Flint Lane. Cross into the conservation area and shadow the wall to the right to the brow. Go through the gate on the right and follow an eroded path up to an unusually large cairn (GR055866) (1h). Bear WNW for 200m to the beacon and then proceed due west over a wall to the top of Penhill Scar. Follow the line of the top of the crag (there is a narrow path), being sure to keep with it by going right of the wall at the fence. Continue above Black Scar to around 100m short of the next wall (GR042866) and then make a very sharp descent – there is no obvious route (beware of the large and small crags along here), but a grassy chute gives the easiest line to level ground. Now shadow the line of a collapsed wall north across some rough, reedy grass to rejoin the path by a gate in the wall. Go through and follow a broad green way down to High Lane. Turn

◄ Penhill Scar

left and follow the hard, wide lane for 1.7km to a fork by Morpeth Scar, turning downhill along an increasingly loose section for 500m to a stile on the right (SP Templars' Chapel) (2h20). Cross into the field and walk along broadly level ground to just above a lengthy wood. Trace a line shadowing the top of the wood to arrive at the ruined preceptory soon after the first walled lane. Continue as before for 2km – crossing another lane midway – to the edge of the road. Bear ESE to a stile up the field and then pass to the south of the small plantation. At the end of the next field, go through the stile to the right before continuing east to the road. Walk beside the A684 through the village back to the lay-by (3h40).

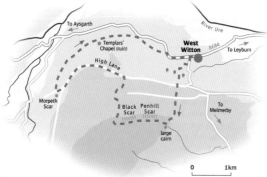

Penhill Preceptory

The Knights Templar – who should need little introduction to readers of *The Da Vinci Code* – were an immensely powerful and wealthy order of soldier-monks established at the time of the crusades to protect and spread Christianity in the Holy Land. They ended up with diverse interests to support their cause, including banking and agriculture, the preceptory at Penhill belonging to around ten estates they maintained in Yorkshire. The ruin here is of the adjoining chapel, which was in existence from around 1202 to the suppression of the order between 1308 and 1312. (The knights' *raison d'etre* vanished with the loss of their footholds in the Holy Land, leaving only a power distrusted by Europe's regal and church authorities.) The Penhill preceptory quickly fell to ruin, no doubt with human help. The remains of the chapel were finally uncovered in 1840.

High on Harker Hill

Walk time 3h20 Height gain 300m
Distance 11km OS Map Explorer OL30

From an invigorating moorland stride by Iron Age earthworks to lazy riverside pastures, spend an entertaining half-day exploring the flavours of Swaledale.

  Start from Reeth village green (parking on the sets and on the green itself) (GR038992). Walk to the southwest corner of the green, through Anvil Square to the alley to the right. At the road, turn left and then right at the end to head down the lane past the doctors' surgery. Follow the path around a sharp left turn, descending to fields and the path to the Swing Bridge. At the far bank, follow the river downstream (southeast) to the first fence — climb the slope beyond to beneath the farmhouse. Pass to the left of it, walk up the farm track to the road and turn left. After 150m join the track (SP Dyke House) rising to the right, continuing up the field after the track

bends sharply left towards the house. Trend left to the southeast corner of the field, cross to the open fell and continue southeast (after 100m be sure to move away from the path by the wall — follow sheepruns through the heather) to a gate by a combined ditch and embankment earthwork. Go through the gate and bear south for 150m, cross a beck and then go back through the fence at a gate to a green track. A gradual ascent leads to a crossroads after 600m — it is straight on here up a stony, slightly steepening track for a further 600m to an impressive earthwork marking the eastern edge of the flat hilltop. Now proceed west with the track over the cratered summit, the barely noticeable top of which lies just to the south of the track after almost 1km (GR018971) (2h). The descent is initially gentle but steepening and turning generally north. After a loss of 120m in height, look for a green track crossing the main route —

◀ Sunrise by the Swing Bridge

turn right. The track quickly dissolves into a very narrow path – perhaps just a sheeprun – contouring ENE through the heather to the site of the Iron Age Maiden Castle fort (it will probably feel further from the track than it actually is – around 1km) (GR021980). It is a short descent north to the road. Bear left and follow it for 600m to a gate on the right – at a section where the wall falls away from the road (SP Grinton). Beyond, a path initially high above the river quickly sweeps down to the waterside, which can then be followed back to the Swing Bridge and the return to Reeth (3h20).

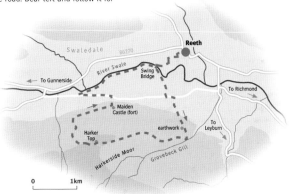

A bridge over troubled water

The rippling Swale may look placid, but beware – it is one of the fastest-flowing rivers in Britain and one of the quickest to rise. The Swing Bridge at Reeth – built in 1920 – nevertheless withstood the worst of its floods and torrents for 80 years. That was until 19 September 2000, when high waters sent an uprooted tree crashing into its middle. The extent of the damage left none of the anchors, cables or stanchions salvageable. Community fundraising and the support of various public bodies saw a £110,000 replacement opened on 29 November 2002 by local MP William Hague. Just to be sure of preventing a repetition, the abutments and cable anchor blocks are now secured into the ground by 6m-long steel piles.

To the Edge

Calver Hill (485m), Fremington Edge
(473m) Walk time 4h15 Height gain 525m
Distance 12.5km OS Map Explorer OL30

**Not many 'Edges' feel like edges, but
along this route Fremington Edge does.
Build up to it with a circuit around lower
Arkengarthdale, including an ascent of
windswept Calver Hill.**

Start from Reeth village green (parking
on the sets and on the green itself)
(GR038992). Walk west out of the village
on the B6270. Some 100m after the last
house, swing right up a narrow walled lane
(SP Skelgate) to its end at the intake wall.
On the open moor, follow the obvious path
contouring west. After around 350m, look

for a faint break in the heather to the right
– leave the path and ascend easily WNW
across rough, heathery terrain, broken by
sheepruns and intermittent tracks, to a
lengthy bield (stone windbreak) pointing
northwest up steeper ground to the summit
cairn on Calver Hill (GR013003) (1h15).
From the top bear west across a shallow
depression to a tiny subsidiary top, then
down a short but steep drop to a green
track. Follow this north to a junction with a
stony vehicle track – turn right. Reaching
the road after almost 1km, descend to Arkle
Town, turning into the cul-de-sac to the
right just past the bridge. Before the last
house cross the stile into the field to the
right (SP Footpath), joining a path to the

riverside. Cross the bridge (2h) and bear right along the walled lane to a pretty, wooded section. At the fork keep left on the higher path (SP Bridleway). Out of the trees, turn right at the next junction of paths (SP Fremington) down to Storthwaite Hall. Past the house, turn through the gateway up the old miners' track. A steady climb leads to the scarred open fell. Keep to the right of the gully (yellow-tipped posts mark the way), then follow the easily graded path on a wide 's' bend. As the ground levels out follow a line of small cairns WSW, veering southeast to the prominent cairn above the crags after around 300m, an excellent vantage point (GR024023) (2h45). Now follow the faint path directly above the 'edge' (ignoring the main cairned path, which quickly leads to the 'wrong' side of the wall to the east) for

a superb, exhilarating walk. After just over 2.5km, descend at a stone track. Cross just above the white house to a path descending steeply through the fields. As the ground levels off, follow the distinct marked route through the pastures east of Arkle Beck to the roadbridge. Cross the bridge and follow the road back up to the green, where traditional forms of refreshment await (4h15).

Sheep story

Sheep are pretty much everywhere in the Dales, and the premier sheep in these parts is the Swaledale. Despite its name, the hardy, black-faced Swaledale is far from exclusive to the dale it was named after, or even the Dales, being found across the North of England. Even so, when the time came to imagine an emblem for the National Park, a Swaledale ram's head it was, replete with horns. Today, that has become an enduring symbol of the area, almost as commonplace as the sheep themselves.

◄ Calver Hill from Harkerside

Arkengarthdale explorations

Great Pinseat (583m) Walk time 4h40
Height gain 385m Distance 15km
OS Map Explorer OL30

**The clue is in the name – Hard Level
Gill. For the lead miners of old this must
have been a crippling place to earn a
living. Today, thankfully, we can wander
across this fascinating, barren moor,
safe in the knowledge that lush
Arkengarthdale awaits and that only our
imaginations have been troubled.**

Start from Langthwaite YDNPA car park
(GR005023). Walk into the village, cross the
bridge and bear right to pick up the
bridleway beside Arkle Beck. After 750m
cross the footbridge back over the beck and
follow the path beyond up to Arkle Town.
Head left past cottages back to the main

road, then walk right for 50m and cross the
stile opposite (SP Fore Gill Gate). The faint
path skirts briefly south around tiny
Cumbers Hill and then rises to gain an
elevated line above the gill. Shadow the
wall running to the right, continuing in the
same direction (southwest) through an open
field to rejoin the wall. Some 100m further
on, drop down into the gill and cross the
wall at the bottom. Bear right and continue
alongside this to Fore Gill Gate; descend to
the road, following it south for 1km as it
undulates gently downhill. Just before
Surrender Bridge, swing onto a broad, solid
track breaking right into Hard Level Gill
(1h20). Running above the northern bank of
the beck, the track makes for easy,
uneventful walking for 1.5km to the well-
preserved remains of Old Gang Smelting

◄ Surrender Bridge

Mills (GR974005). Continue, gradually gaining height, to reach Level House Bridge after a further 1.4km – do not cross the bridge, instead stick with the track next to the gill as the moor opens out and a certain desolate beauty unfurls. Beyond a gate, bear east with the track into a lunar, spoiled landscape; 800m on, approaching a particularly large cairn/spoil heap, traverse north over rough ground to the wall. Follow this east to quickly reach a breach with the summit trig point just beyond (GR970027) (3h). Now forge a way north through heather for 250m to a green track. Bear east, taking the left (lower) fork after 350m. So begins a wonderful descent along a

springy green (and initially zigzagging) track to the spoil heap at Danby Level. Once there, split east along an equally fine path, continuing straight through another area of spoil to reach the road. Turn left and follow it for 250m to a gate on the right. Descend, trending right through this and a subsequent field to a footbridge over Arkle Beck (4h). Cross and head downstream; 100m before the stone roadbridge head back over the beck at a footbridge and resume; cross the road and follow the farm track opposite to a lane, turning left. By the cottages bear right down the church lane to the main road – a short hop now leads back to the car park (4h40).

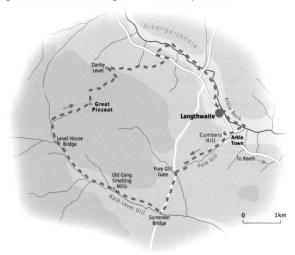

Two sides of Swaledale

Walk time 5h30 Height gain 470m
Distance 17km OS Map Explorer OL30

From the scarred grandeur of Gunnerside Gill to the pastoral, airy beauty of Ivelet Side: two faces of Upper Swaledale and one of the Dales' best days.

Start from the parking area beside the bridge in the middle of Gunnerside (GR950982). Cross to the eastern side of the bridge and follow the beck upstream. Skirt around the large house at the end of the village into the fields beyond. Entering woods, the path rises to an elevated line winding between the trees. Emerging, beckside pastures lead to the remains of Sir Francis Level, the first of many relics of lead mining to encounter. The path now steadily climbs to a green terrace contouring north to the spectacularly scarred workings by Bunton Hush (1h). Continue along the terrace for a further 350m – as it begins to dip, break right on a path ascending

through scree. This quickly fades into a faint moorland path bending back to the southeast to gain a wide track – resume north, shadowing the gill below. Pass a shooting hut, then – 100m on – take the track forking left. After 300m, as the track bends right, bear west the short distance down to the modest Blakethwaite Dam (GR934029) (2h). Remain on the northern bank and follow the beck downstream (ignore the muddy crossing) to reach a solid path descending from the east. Coming to a ruined mine building, cross the beck and continue down the gill on another good path to the smelting mill at the foot of the Blind Gill ravine. Cross the beck from Blind Gill, walk south for 100m, then turn directly up to the right along a narrow path switching first back towards Blind Gill, then southwest across a gradually easing gradient to a track by the workings at Lownathwaite (GR931013). Bear west and crest the open moor – a dramatic change

◀ Gunnerside Gill workings

after the enclosed gill. Descend for 750m, leave the track by the footpath signpost and keep right to follow the northern bank of East Grain. A steep and intermittently rocky descent into the cleft of the gill leads to (another) ruined smelting mill with a notable view down Swinner Gill (GR912012) (3h30). Return a few metres upstream and cross to a narrow path traversing the hillside south. The path weaves along a terrace, with wonderful open views, broken only by the twin indents of West Arn Gill and Arn Gill. Beyond the latter, the route climbs slightly and narrows to a shelf arcing above a sharp slope and patches of scree. Soon enough this opens out to a broad green path, first beneath Kisdon Scar and then above Cock Crow Scar, before gradually descending east to the road above

Ivelet (5h). Continue downhill, and then turn right down the steep road past Gunnerside Lodge into the hamlet. Turn left by the signposts for the 'Estate Office' and 'Footpath Gunnerside', dropping down to cross the wooded beck beyond the office before following the easy route east through the meadows back to Gunnerside (5h30).

What's a Hush?

Bunton Hush, Frairfold Hush, North Hush, Lownathwaite Hush – there is no shortage of Hushes in Gunnerside Gill. 'Hushing' was a process to extract lead ore from close to the surface – a stream would be dammed, allowing an accumulation of water to build behind; at the desired moment this was then breached, the force of the rushing water sweeping away the overlying peat and loose rock to expose the ore beneath. At least, that was the idea. Repeated this left huge gashes in the landscape and exposed vast quantities of scree, the 'Hushes'. A relatively cheap and easy form of extraction, the Hushes pre-date the more sophisticated Levels (tunnelled shafts tracing veins into the hillside).

Beyond Kisdon

Kisdon (499m), **Clumpstone Hill** (441m)
Walk time 5h30 Height gain 470m
Distance 18km OS Map Explorer OL30

**Take that charming – and popular –
objective Kisdon, the finest small hill in
the Dales. Take the rough, untouched
country beyond, over Clumpstone Hill
and through Whitsundale. Combine the
varied ingredients (rounded out by a
magical riverside return to Muker) and
you have a day to remember.**

Start from the YDNPA car park by Muker
(GR910978). Walk into the village – turn up
by the green; then back on the level, wind
first left, then right between the cottages to
pick up a walled lane. Pass a couple of final
houses to a gate, beyond which an initially

metalled track zigzags up the hillside.
As the track bends left through a gateway,
continue up the green lane ahead. Now
shadow the wall to the left to enter another
enclosed section. As the field opens out,
keep with the wall to the right as it bends
back west to reach the summit plateau. An
obvious way leads WNW, turning beyond
the next gate (GR897992) to the north for a
gradual descent across springy grass, with
great views opening out west over Angram.
Merge with a stone track above a small
wood, following this over a ford to the road.
Turn left and then left into the field after
100m. Follow a path SSW through a
succession of tiny pastures; 300m after
crossing Ay Gill, join the shelf rising back
up to the road just to the left of a

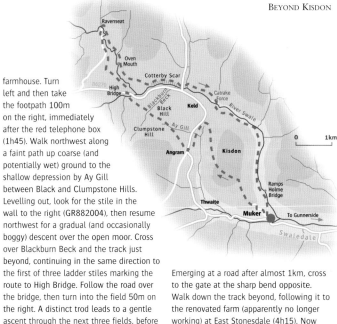

farmhouse. Turn left and then take the footpath 100m on the right, immediately after the red telephone box (1h45). Walk northwest along a faint path up coarse (and potentially wet) ground to the shallow depression by Ay Gill between Black and Clumpstone Hills. Levelling out, look for the stile in the wall to the right (GR882004), then resume northwest for a gradual (and occasionally boggy) descent over the open moor. Cross over Blackburn Beck and the track just beyond, continuing in the same direction to the first of three ladder stiles marking the route to High Bridge. Follow the road over the bridge, then turn into the field 50m on the right. A distinct trod leads to a gentle ascent through the next three fields, before a traverse north over a depression and a contour around to a single-track road. Bear right and follow this to its conclusion at Ravenseat. Cross the bridge ahead, walk into the farmyard and cross the stile to the right by the signpost for Keld (3h15). A gently rising path returns south to above the spectacular gorge at Oven Mouth (GR868022). Here, be sure to take the lower of the two paths (beneath the sheepfold) across some damp terrain to join a stone track by an abandoned farmhouse. After 400m, just before the last wall on the left, break left to pick up a narrow path running east along the top of Cotterby Scar.

Emerging at a road after almost 1km, cross to the gate at the sharp bend opposite. Walk down the track beyond, following it to the renovated farm (apparently no longer working) at East Stonesdale (4h15). Now descend along the Pennine Way track, turning down again before Catrake Force. Cross the footbridge over the Swale and climb the steps rising right to a junction with another path. Here, turn left to traverse through the woods; after 300m bear left at the fork in the path (SP Muker). Gradually emerging from the trees, drop with the path down to handsome riverside pastures (though the path is only relatively briefly next to the water). Keep with the Swale to the reinforced section just before Ramps Holme Bridge. Cross the stile to the right and follow the paved path the short distance back into Muker (5h30).

◀ Angram field patterns from Kisdon

Index

Addlebrough	80	Great Pinseat	90	Pennine Way	
Angram Reservoir	8	Great Shunner Fell	72		40, 48, 72, 74, 94
Appletreewick	16	Great Whernside	32	Plover Hill	40
Arant Haw	64	Green Bell	68	Randygill Top	68
Arkengarthdale	88, 90	Grere Fell	68	Raydale	76
Arkle Town	88, 90	Gunnerside Gill	92	Reeth	86, 88
Arncliffe	28, 30	Halton Gill	38, 40	Ribblehead Viaduct	56
Austwick	46	Harker Hill	86	Ribblesdale	42, 44, 48
Aysgarth	82	Hawes	74	Scar House Reservoir	8
Bainbridge	76	Hebden	18	Sedbergh	64
Beezley Falls	52	Horse Head	38	Semer Water	76
Benfoot Brow	20	Horton	48, 50	Settle	44
Blackfell Crags	32	Howgills	60, 64, 66, 68	Settle-Carlisle Railway	56
Bolton Abbey	12	Hubberholme	36	Simon's Seat	14
Bolton Castle	82	Ingleborough	50, 52	Sleddale	74
Buckden	30, 34, 36	Ingleton	52, 54	Smearsett Scar	44
Buckden Pike	34	Kensgriff	68	Sulber Nick	50
Burnsall	16	Kettlewell	30, 32	Swaledale	78, 86, 92
Calders	64	Kingsdale	54	Swarth Fell	70
Calf, The	64	Kisdon	94	Thornton Rust	80
Calver Hill	88	Langstrothdale	36, 38	Three Peaks	
Castle Bolton	82	Langthwaite	90		42, 48, 50, 52, 58
Cautley Crag	66, 68	Linton	22	Thwaite	94
Combe Scar	62	Litton	30	Tor Dyke	32
Crummackdale	46	Littondale	24, 28, 30, 38	Troller's Gill	16
Dales Way	20, 30, 38	Lofthouse	8	Twistleton Scar	52, 54
Deepdale	38, 58	Malham	24, 26	Valley of Desolation	14
Dent	58, 62	Malham Tarn	28	Wensleydale	74, 80, 82
Dentdale	56, 58, 62	Mastiles Lane	22	West Witton	84
Dodd Fell	74	Middle Hare Head	12	Wharfedale	6, 14, 16, 20,
Drumaldrace	74	Mossdale Scar	20		22, 24, 30, 32, 34, 36
Fremington Edge	88	Moughton Scar	46	Whernside	58
Gaping Gill	50	Muker	94	Whitsundale	94
Gordale Scar	26	Nidderdale	6, 8	Wild Boar Fell	70
Grassington	20, 22	Occupation Road	62	Yarlside	68
Great Dummacks	66	Pateley Bridge	10	Yockenthwaite	36, 38
Great Knoutberry Hill	56	Pen-y-ghent	40, 48	Yorke's Folly	10